Proposal Writing for Nursing Capstones and Clinical Projects

Wanda Bonnel, PhD, GNP-BC, ANEF, is associate professor at the University of Kansas School of Nursing, Kansas City, Kansas. As a specialist in geriatrics and nursing education, she teaches courses in the master's, doctor of nursing practice (DNP), and doctoral programs, including advanced clinical residency and a capstone course for DNPs. She is a fellow in the National League for Nursing Academy and recipient of the Chancellor's Distinguished Teaching Award at the University of Kansas, and received the Sigma Theta Tau Regional Pinnacle Award for computer-based professional education technology. Dr. Bonnel has received multiple funded grants, including the Health Resources and Services Administration (HRSA) online Health Professions Educator Certificate program. She has published numerous peer-reviewed abstracts and articles in geriatric and educator specialty journals, including *Clinical Advisor* and *Journal of Professional Nursing*. She coauthored the textbook *Teaching Technologies in Nursing and the Health Professions* (2010). Her ongoing research interests include online learning best practices and advanced practice mentoring. Dr. Bonnel has served as grant reviewer for the National League for Nursing and HRSA and a manuscript reviewer for selected journals, and is an editorial board member of the *Journal of Gerontological Nursing*. Her current work in the DNP advanced clinical and capstone courses provides valuable background and opportunity to identify selected student-learning needs for this text.

Katharine V. Smith, PhD, RN, ACNS-BC, CNE, is associate professor and assistant dean for program evaluation at the University of Missouri, Kansas City School of Nursing. Dr. Smith has received multiple grants, most of which have focused on aspects of teaching, advanced education, and nursing traineeships. Recent scholarship includes peer-reviewed publications and national presentations on the use of simulation to teach legal and ethical content. She has also coauthored the textbook *Teaching Technologies in Nursing and the Health Professions* (2010). Dr. Smith teaches in both the undergraduate and the graduate nursing programs, facilitating advanced clinical projects through the institutional review board process. She also conducts program review and site visits for both nursing and non-nursing programs and serves as a consultant editor for the *Nursing Ethics* journal.

Proposal Writing for Nursing Capstones and Clinical Projects

WANDA BONNEL, PhD, GNP-BC, ANEF
KATHARINE V. SMITH, PhD, RN, ACNS-BC, CNE

SPRINGER PUBLISHING COMPANY
NEW YORK

Springer Publishing Company, LLC
11 West 42nd Street
New York, NY 10036
www.springerpub.com

Acquisitions Editor: Margaret Zuccarini
Composition: diacriTech

ISBN: 978-0-8261-2288-9
e-book ISBN: 978-0-8261-0863-0

14 15 16 / 5 4

The author and the publisher of this Work have made every effort to use sources believed to be reliable to provide information that is accurate and compatible with the standards generally accepted at the time of publication. The author and publisher shall not be liable for any special, consequential, or exemplary damages resulting, in whole or in part, from the readers' use of, or reliance on, the information contained in this book. The publisher has no responsibility for the persistence or accuracy of URLs for external or third-party Internet websites referred to in this publication and does not guarantee that any content on such websites is, or will remain, accurate or appropriate.

Library of Congress Cataloging-in-Publication Data

Bonnel, Wanda E.
  Proposal writing for nursing capstones and clinical projects / Wanda Bonnel, Katharine V. Smith.
    p. ; cm.
  Includes bibliographical references and index.
  ISBN 978-0-8261-2288-9—ISBN 0-8261-2288-4—ISBN 978-0-8261-0863-0 (e-book)
  I. Smith, Katharine Vogel. II. Title.
  [DNLM: 1. Clinical Nursing Research. 2. Research Design. 3. Writing. WY 20.5]
  RT71
  610.73076—dc23
                           2013014394

Printed in the United States of America by Gasch Printing.

Contents

Contributors for Proposal Abstracts and Project Examples

Karri Arndt, DNP, APRN   University of Kansas, Nurse Anesthesia Education, Kansas City, Kansas

Paula Israel, DNP, APRN-BC   University of Kansas School of Nursing, Kansas City, Kansas

Linda Kroeger, DNP(c), APRN   University of Kansas School of Nursing, Kansas City, Kansas

Roberta Mansfield, DNP, FNP-BC   Washburn University School of Nursing, Topeka, Kansas

Preface

As new graduate programs evolve at schools across the country, diverse student cohorts have the opportunity to enhance their skill sets in planning and writing proposals. This book shares the "must know" for gaining a set of clinical scholarship tools for writing a concise, scholarly project proposal. The purpose of the text is to provide practical guides for graduate students and advanced clinicians to organize and package their clinical projects through tight proposals.

The concept of advanced clinical projects is described broadly. All health care professionals, whether they are in direct or indirect practice roles, are, in essence, seeking to provide improved health outcomes for populations and quality, efficient patient care. This uniqueness provides an opportunity to raise awareness of diverse important problems or concerns in various practice areas.

A well-written clinical project proposal is a form of scholarly communication and is expected in advanced practice. The text is broadly written to support diverse clinical project topics. Although the uniqueness of advanced nursing practice allows no one proposal "formula," there are guides for taking unique topics and relating these to common project models. Focus is on the use of the best evidence in projects, including synthesis of the literature for further project work.

Gaining ongoing skills for quality improvement, evaluation, and collaborative research is valued. Although clinical projects can have similarities to theses and dissertations in some cases, the clinical project proposals are much more focused on gaining best evidence for use in advancing quality patient care. So often the tools of research will be used in writing proposals, but the focus of the clinical project is to gain best use of evidence for improving clinical care. This book guides the reader in using tools gained in previous courses, such as theory, research, and statistics, to develop a sound proposal for a quality advanced clinical project. The "must know" information from these courses is reinforced, and references for further reading are recommended.

Much of a good clinical project proposal relates to being a reflective clinician and thinking prospectively of the big picture of the project, from start to finish, so important parts are not missed. A toolkit of resources, including a project triangle framework, guides graduate students and clinicians in practical skills for proposal planning and writing. Using a reflective clinician approach, guidelines and checklists are provided to develop quality capstone proposals. Students interact with the content through the ongoing reflective prompts and questions to guide them in reflective writing to better understand their projects and what they propose to do. The following broad themes organize the 15 chapters in a logical flow toward completion of planning and writing a clinical project proposal.

1. Writing Your Proposal: Putting Your "Problem" in Context. Putting a clinical problem in context, including an introduction to the topic and problem statement, is important in making the case for and outlining a project. Context also includes synthesizing the literature on a clinical topic and placing a project within that existing literature.

2. Writing Your Proposal: Designing and Setting the Stage for Your Project. The key points of a scholarly methods section that flows from a purpose statement are considered. Consistent with the methods of the sciences, traditional research methods are discussed as tools for capstone projects.

3. Writing Your Proposal: Adding the Detail for Proposal Completion. The importance of visualizing the finished product, editing for concise, understandable language, and fine-tuning proposal methods and analyses are all considered.

This book provides students with tools to implement in their own scholarly practice. Key features to engage readers include the following: chapter objectives, tips for making proposals complete and concise, and key point summaries. Reflective questions, exemplars, and activities for the reader are included. This text helps develop reflective clinical scholars who can write about clinical challenges, propose solutions, and use the methods of science to develop scholarly proposals.

Wanda Bonnel, PhD, GNP-BC, ANEF
Katharine V. Smith, PhD, RN, ACNS-BC, CNE

Acknowledgments

The authors acknowledge the many individuals who have influenced the writing of this book. We thank our students who continue to help us learn, our university colleagues for sharing ongoing discussions and ideas, and program graduates who have shared resources for chapter examples. Additionally, we thank our families for their ongoing encouragement and patience as we worked on this book. Thank you also to our Springer Publishing Company colleagues, especially Chris Teja and Margaret Zuccarini, for encouragement in this text development.

1

Introduction: Why a Scholarly Proposal for the Clinical Project Proposal?

REFLECTIVE QUESTIONS

As you begin your work on a clinical project proposal, there are benefits to reflecting on your goals. You have ideas for the clinical project and are seeking further thoughts for turning these ideas into scholarly proposals that will lead to tight, strong, finished projects. The following reflective questions will help you consider your writing plan and organize learning for this chapter. Which of the following do you have the most comfort responding to?

- What makes a project proposal important?
- What does it mean to write a clinical project proposal?
- How do concepts of reflective clinician and clinical scholarship relate?
- What makes a clinical proposal scholarly?
- How does best evidence fit with clinical projects?
- What are common terms related to best evidence and clinical project proposals?

PROPOSAL WRITING FOR SCHOLARLY CLINICAL PROJECTS: THE IMPORTANCE

This book is designed to help you become a reflective clinical scholar and write proposals for clinical projects that impact patient care. Clinical scholarship is key to advancing patient care and at this time of change in health care, advanced clinical nursing scholarship is needed more than ever. Your important role in becoming a clinical scholar continues to increase as you learn to write proposals for clinical projects. A clinical project proposal can help name one aspect of what you do as an advanced clinician and plan a project that positively impacts that aspect of your practice.

The concept of project design is key in proposal development. Design, as a broad concept, is often considered a tool for making things better. Designers can be considered agents of change. As an advanced clinician, you will be assessing current situations and in many cases proposing a change process for improving clinical outcomes. As proposal designer, the clinical project proposal can be one step in this development.

WRITING A CLINICAL PROJECT PROPOSAL

A proposal is a straightforward, logically organized, clear document that includes essential details that will guide a project. A proposal is considered the plan for how work will be designed to learn something important related to an interest area. Proposals are further described as a presentation of ideas, a study justification, and a work plan, which serve as evidence of a chain of reasoning, project feasibility, and binding contract for proposed work (Krathwohl & Smith, 2005). The proposal plan needs to be logical, with the overall plan flowing from a problem statement. It demonstrates how a need is met by this project and how it builds on previous work to address that need.

Scholarly clinical projects are one way you, as the advanced clinician, gain opportunities for making practice more visible to the public. Project aims can include promoting better patient care, supporting healthy people and community initiatives, and contributing to quality improvement in health care systems. The specific purpose of your clinical project may relate to addressing patient care outcomes that are about safety, quality care, quality of life, or patient transitions. As an advanced clinical practice nurse and leader, you develop clinical projects that integrate best evidence and consider contributions from other disciplines for the purpose of improving clinical practice.

The proposal is a written portion of the scholarly clinical project that "proposes" what is to be done to complete that project. It also situates the project within the existing literature on the topic. Once the proposal for the clinical project is approved, the clinical project is ready to be implemented. Once the proposed activities are completed, the proposal document then is adapted to become the final project summary. To complete the final summary paper, the proposal methods are changed to past tense (in other words completed), and new sections on project results and implications are added. Thus, this is a useful, versatile document that:

1. Serves as a form of communication or as a type of information sharing.
2. Proposes what is to be done (provides the plan or proposed project outline to be implemented) so others can understand, provide approval, or even replicate.
3. Identifies important, related literature.
4. Provides information in a written and scholarly format through which others can quickly find key concepts.
5. Serves as a type of contract identifying clear expectations for a class or program requirement.
6. Serves as the basis for becoming a final project document that integrates the project proposal and outcomes.

This book guides you through steps for naming what you plan to do and describing to others how you plan to do it. For example, the Institute of Medicine (IOM; 2012) has identified the need for leadership in chronic care management. Advanced nurses have the opportunity to address population health issues to improve public health. Approaches such as education and quality improvement can be considered to help manage or control a chronic illness for a population subset. Designing a related clinical project could involve the following: naming a specific chronic illness and problem (such as osteoarthritis and pain management), selecting related concepts for further development or study that would lead to improved pain management (such as patient group coaching sessions on lifestyle modifications), reviewing the literature to determine the status of the evidence on the proposed concept, and finally framing this into a proposal for implementing or testing the best evidence to improve care of patients with osteoarthritis pain.

CLINICAL SCHOLARSHIP AND THE REFLECTIVE CLINICIAN

Clinical Scholarship

Boyer (1990) described the importance of acknowledging clinical scholarship as well as sophisticated research programs. His classic framework for documenting scholarship includes frames of teaching, application, integration, and discovery. He provides a model for helping professionals not only share clinical products with others, but to reflect on and continue to improve these clinical products. Quality-improvement projects provide a good example of this process. Projects that serve as a type of quality improvement can help others know and learn from your observations and experiences. To meet the scholarship definition, components of product documentation, peer review, and publication or dissemination are required (Hutchings, 2002).

The Benefits of Reflection

Being an expert clinician or clinical leader comes with the responsibility of reflecting on practice issues to advance clinical patient care solutions. Reflection is a strategy that allows one to pause and think about what is going on; what is working or not working in a clinical or work-related situation. Reflection serves as a way to assess or identify gaps in clinical practice and move forward in clinical practice. Learning from these assessments often provides direction for future projects. As these ideas move to clinical project proposals, scholarly products and conversation that lead to clinical scholarship continue.

Critique of the current status of a particular care situation, for example, fall prevention, could involve addressing the problem from a systems perspective. This could incorporate reflection on the current unit or practice site structures and processes (both needs and gaps) for gaining positive outcomes. Listening, observing, and writing about this situation provide a starting point for related project development. In this situation a reflective clinician asks, What is the team doing? How is it working? What could be better? These questions then lead to the opportunity for future clinical projects.

Scholarly writing is also related to reflection and scholarly dialogue; this scholarly dialogue involves reading the literature, communicating with others about that literature, and then developing your own scholarly proposal. Further reflection and scholarly dialogue occur with completed project proposals, implementation of the projects, and finally sharing this scholarship via the literature. Scholarly writing of proposals and further products includes using methods of science and the language of the profession for disseminating clinical projects. Again, the scholarly proposal provides written communication to others. It communicates what you will do for the project and later it will be revised to communicate what you did. It provides the basis for a tight scholarly project that can be shared with others.

MAKING A CLINICAL PROPOSAL SCHOLARLY

Writing a scholarly proposal is part of a skill set for furthering clinical scholarship. Scholarly proposals provide a way to share, in a written and professional format, the important points of a major project. The proposal conveys not only what you will do, but why it is important that other people think about this topic. Your proposal summarizes your plans, provides you a road map for implementing plans, and delivers to others a plan that they can review and critique and approve. Scholarly proposals, and then completed projects, provide a means to contribute to the body of knowledge and improve clinical practice.

In your scholarly proposal you will use the language of science and a commonly accepted format for organizing project proposals and final papers. This consistency in structure promotes ease of communication within nursing and the larger, interdisciplinary community. The common sections for a scholarly proposal are:

- Introduction with Problem Summary and Purpose Statement
- Literature Review
- Project Methods

Although clinical project topics are quite variable, in all cases a proposal is an important component and serves as a project guide. In some ways completing a proposal is like putting together a puzzle and making sure all the pieces fit to give the best final picture. A scholarly proposal involves justifying and writing about your plan so that all of the clinical project pieces fit together.

Proposals are important in serving as a mechanism of clear communication about a proposed project. In a clinical and interprofessional world, you will be communicating professionally in the literature and via conference presentations. Scholarly proposals incorporate the language of science with agreed-on terminology for communication. Common agreement across disciplines dictates that scholarly proposals include clear presentation of problem summary, project purpose, literature review, project methods, and projected outcomes. Though this sounds simple, there are numerous components to both consider and address to make this happen. Although this book lays out components by chapter, it is important to consider the back-and-forth nature of each, for example, detailing the problem as a component of reviewing the literature. The art of scholarly proposing, in simple terms, includes:

- Taking an important problem
- Situating that problem in the literature and best evidence

- Framing it into a useful project, in writing, from which others can learn
- Making that written project proposal scholarly and doable

HOW DOES THE REFLECTIVE CLINICIAN USE EVIDENCE IN CLINICAL PROJECTS?

Scholarly dialogue includes reviewing best evidence in the literature as well as other professional sources of best evidence. Considering the state of the evidence can lead to further focusing on the clinical problem. As you move forward in your proposal, you will begin asking questions that help you address how you will

- further understand your concept
- gain a process for evidence-based practice
- enhance quality care
- generate questions requiring further study

Once you have a beginning understanding of what is available in the literature or best evidence, then you are able to make decisions on the type of project that will be most needed related to your problem/topic. This allows you to focus broadly on using the evidence in advanced clinical projects such as the following:

- Synthesizing the literature on topics to develop current best-practice summaries or protocols for testing. An example would be sharing a synthesis of best evidence and protocol for promoting best anesthesia care for pediatric patients dealing with obesity.
- Using and evaluating current best-evidence protocols to implement quality-improvement projects with unique populations. An example would be teaching and evaluating use of an evidence-based protocol on diabetes management in long-term care settings.
- Contributing to the evidence by sharing new clinical data. An example would be surveying rural advanced practice nurses related to their challenges and strategies for dealing with common rural population issues.

COMMON TERMS RELATED TO CLINICAL PROJECTS AND USE OF BEST EVIDENCE

Common terms such as translation of the evidence, research utilization, and evidence-based practice can relate to clinical projects and proposals. Many terms are used in discussing clinical activities based on the evidence. Although there is overlap in these terms, each has unique components:

> *Translation of the evidence*: Translating evidence to knowledge for practice and helping staff become aware of and access evidence-based resources.
>
> *Research utilization*: Applying relevant studies to practice, after specific review and critique of each study.
>
> *Evidence-based practice*: Expanding the concept of research utilization to include not only appropriate research in practice but, when limited research evidence is available, other sources of best evidence such as expert clinician are also considered. The patient preference for treatment is also a component.

Also, the concepts of research, evaluation, and quality improvement are often discussed together. Again, there are similarities and differences in these basic terms as well as frequent overlap of concepts/methods used.

> *Evaluation*: Evaluative projects include systematic methods that judge the effectiveness of specific practices or policies.
>
> *Research*: Large-scale projects that involve systematic inquiry, using specified, disciplined methods of science in addressing problems or questions (Polit & Beck, 2012).
>
> *Quality improvement*: Projects that analyze a system's performance and ways to improve using a formal approach with systematic methods (Duke University, 2005).

Relevant to these concepts, evaluation is a broad project approach/ method used in both research and quality improvement. Research studies typically build in more controls to be more generalizable to other settings and populations. Quality improvement is typically considered more narrow in focus and for specific institutional use.

CLINICAL SCHOLARSHIP: SEEKING AND GAINING A MENTOR

Seeking and gaining a mentor in the early stage of your work is an important and sometimes challenging task. Potential mentors should have expertise specific to content, settings, and methods. A mentor's time availability, the interest to help, and a strong commitment to your professional development are also important. The benefits of having a mentor are many, but in particular include helping you avoid pitfalls in feasibility or effectiveness of clinical project methods. When seeking a mentor, consider concepts of mutual readiness, opportunity, and resources for support. For example, if your mentor is at a distance, are methods available to facilitate conversations, and are both of you mutually interested in participating?

Finding a project mentor and using your project mentor(s) well are beneficial in all phases/aspects of project proposal development, as well as project implementation, evaluation, and completion. Consider the following strategies to seek a mentor or improve current work with a mentor:

- Focus on clear guides and expectations for both mentor and mentee.
- Establish regular meeting times (phone/face to face/electronic).
- Find out when your mentor is available to read reports and what type of feedback your mentor is willing to give. Also ask about the lead time required to review documents.
- Build a schedule for project reports or updates.
- Follow-up on mentor's comments or suggestions.
- If your mentor is at a distance, discuss electronic communication strategies.

INTRODUCTION TO THE CLINICAL PROJECT TRIANGLE

As you move forward with your clinical project, you will want to consider the benefits of a clinical project triangle (Appendix A) and rubric (Appendix B). The three points of the triangle include the project purpose, the methods, and the outcomes. This triangle helps hold the project together from a big-picture perspective and makes the project a cohesive whole. It is useful to begin a proposal with the triangle points in mind (subject to change as literature is reviewed and plans are finalized). For example, in a sample communications project (Appendix C), the purpose was seeking outcomes of improved communication between nursing staff and providers. Methods were then selected that could help achieve the designated outcomes. As noted, the purpose was broad and the methods and outcomes were quite specific. The goal is for all project points on the triangle to mesh so that all aspects of the project are consistent and the overall project is coherent.

SUMMARY

Clinicians have opportunities to impact patient care in changing health care systems. Being an expert clinician or clinical leader comes with the responsibility of reflecting on practice issues and advancing clinical patient care solutions via scholarly projects. Clinical project proposals provide a way to begin naming your specific concepts. Proposals for clinical projects directed at solving clinical problems can be implemented and shared as a form of scholarly practice.

TIPS FOR GETTING STARTED

- Schedule regular times to reflect on a problem topic of interest for your project. Initially avoid getting bogged down in detail. Note and relate facts, your reactions and feelings, and note both frustrations and "aha" moments (Zachary, 2000).
- Add something to your reflections each scheduled time. Even if you are not productive at first, it establishes the routine and sets the expectation to help you develop a regular work pattern.
- Prepare to address the questions your reflections raise: What is the evidence on this topic of interest? What is the state of current practice in a specified location or population? What value is there in further addressing this problem?

NEXT CHAPTER UP

Chapter 2 provides practical guides for getting started with your writing plan. The chapter addresses gaining ideas and tips for writing, asking the right questions, and making good choices to craft project proposals.

LEARNING ACTIVITIES

Beginning Writing Prompts

Writing prompts provide a way to reflect and get some ideas on paper. Use these prompts to brainstorm possibilities.

1. Some of the big concerns I have with my clinical work relate to the following . . .
2. If there is one clinical or work-related problem I would fix, it would be . . . the outcomes I would be interested in would include . . .
3. The people and place factors that impact this problem are . . .
4. If I could focus on just one aspect of this problem, it would be . . .

Writing an Initial Reflection

Begin a written reflection by sharing what has shaped your ideas about a specific topic/problem. What have been your experiences or lessons learned? Then question how these might be similar or different from others' perspectives?

CHECKLIST AND GOAL SETTING: READINESS TO BEGIN A CLINICAL PROJECT

On a scale of 1 to 3 (high), how would you rate yourself on each of the following? What further goals need to be addressed?

At this point in time . . .

1. I am motivated to help improve patient outcomes via advanced clinical projects.
2. I have beginning clinical challenges/ideas I would like to further develop.
3. I am in a situation that supports moving forward with a clinical project.
4. I am ready to communicate professionally via a written proposal.

2

Using the Writing Plan as a Developmental Tool for the Advanced Clinical Project

REFLECTIVE QUESTIONS

In Chapter 1 your focus was thinking about what you do as a clinician and beginning to identify where clinical improvements are needed. You considered the importance of your scholarly project proposal. The following reflective questions organize learning for this chapter. Which of the following do you have the most comfort with?

- Why is this writing plan important? What makes clinical scholarship and proposal writing go together?
- What does it mean to organize and draft a writing plan? Why a self-directed learning and writing focus?
- What are strategies to begin and keep the scholarly writing plans moving forward?

A good clinical project, written first as a clinical proposal, guides and enhances project quality for credible outcomes. Reflective clinicians begin a proposal by seeing a problem, generating a plan for dealing with the problem through the proposal process, and then implementing this clinical project. Reflective clinicians, as self-directed writers, follow steps that guide the proposal write-up, taking ideas and meshing them with project guidelines or templates for quality projects.

A written proposal is the first formal step of a clinical project and is a form of clinical scholarship. This chapter is about organizing and getting started with the writing plan. It is also about being a reflective clinician and sharing through writing. This chapter moves you forward in considering reading and writing together, gaining a plan for self-directed writing, drafting a scholarly writing plan, and strategies to keep the scholarly writing process moving along.

CONSIDERING SCHOLARLY WRITING AND READING TOGETHER

Writing as a Tool in Gaining a Good Problem and Project Approaches

The goal is to write a proposal that names clearly your project plans. This accomplishes two things: (1) it allows you to clarify what you will be doing and (2) it provides a map or guide so that others can understand the merit of the project and replicate the project in other settings. You can begin drafting a plan by answering questions that include: Who am I writing for? Who is my audience? What are the rules? As you name and learn about specific clinical issues of interest, you are reflecting and writing about them.

Linking Scholarly Writing With Reading

At this stage in the clinical project, reading and writing fit together. While reading, you are gaining a big picture of the topic and planning how to situate your specific issue within its appropriate context (including both its setting and available literature in the area). This involves gaining an orientation to your topic and evidence-based resources.

- Use active reading to narrow the field (preview articles and consider questions to address further in reading).
- As you read, look for questions about studies and findings: who, what, where, how large, and how are outcomes gained?

Typically you have focused on reading to learn more about specific practice concepts. At this point you are also reading to consider approaches that might be used to help move your clinical project forward. What do you learn from what others have done that can be used to package projects in meaningful ways to benefit colleagues, staff, and students?

A PLAN FOR SELF-DIRECTED WRITING:
PREWRITING AND THE BROAD WRITING PLAN

Why should you care about the writing plan? Because a limited plan typically means a limited product. Because you have limited hours, you have to maximize your use of those hours. The writing plan is important because it helps outline the important points and makes writing a central tool. Just as planning in nursing is central to patient care, the larger clinical project can be considered to take a similar "care plan" approach in assessing project need, clearly stating the problem, outlining possible approaches, and then selecting best for the situation. This includes evaluation to determine how the project plan is working.

Prewriting occurs before official proposal writing starts. This is when you get organized and ready to write. It can include getting yourself to your writing place; sticking to the time you allotted; having a beverage in hand; and getting sufficient reading, thinking, and exploring done to lead your writing down the right path (putting together reading notes in a way that can later be cited is also useful).

Prewriting also provides an opportunity for early organization of thoughts or to clarify problems, as well as to help identify what your project is not about (Wolcott, 2008). Because this prewriting helps focus your ideas, the project becomes more reasonable and then becomes a more do-able project. Your actual problem can become clearer through this process. It provides opportunities to consider other phases of the work.

Sometimes reflecting on broad questions serves as a good prewriting tool. For example, why is this topic interesting to me? Specific writing tools such as project decision trails or reflective journals help you document your work, reflecting and journaling to help assess what is working or not with your project plans. Writing and critical thinking make a good connection. Getting-started tips for organizing a writing plan, including your writing time and space, consist of:

- When to write? When thinking about your time organization, does your plan involve a calendar/a clock? Are you a morning or night person? What's compatible with your personal and family life?
- Where to write? Your writing space counts too. Do you require a quiet, peaceful place to write or can you write anywhere? Often selecting one central writing area, with organized supplies and resources, helps writing efficiency. An added bonus is finding a spot where you can spread out and not have to pick up every time after you have finished working.
- What to write? Anything; just start to get something on paper. Then work into the specific proposal components you are addressing.

Tips to Maintain Momentum for Your Writing Plan

Many life events will distract from your writing. Try to put writing first for selected time periods (other than emergencies). Tips for keeping momentum up include:

- Develop a big-picture project map that helps you stay on track.
- Be realistic in goal setting or do-ability of plans; describe deliverables.
- Organize tasks with a timeline and check it regularly.
- Be clear and enthusiastic about goals.
- Identify a mentor or colleague support person.
- Identify someone besides yourself to whom you're responsible for accomplishing specified work and meeting due dates.

DRAFTING THE SCHOLARLY WRITING PLAN

Organization is important and different for scholarly proposals than it is for other types of writing. While textbooks are written for broad audiences to highlight and summarize key content areas, in a clinical proposal, the format becomes more prescriptive. For example, at least three focused sections are addressed in scholarly proposals, including the introduction (with problem summary and project purpose statement), literature review, and methods. Specific sections, such as the methods section, then address further project components (project design, sample, data collection, and data-analysis plans). Future chapters will address these topics.

To begin organizing the scholarly writing plan, reflective questions and written responses can help make the connections to puzzling problems. Sample questions include the following:

- *What will you be doing?* When writing the scholarly proposal, there are multiple concepts to consider. This will include writing what is known about your problem or clinical project topic and writing the literature review (what others have done). You will also be writing about the plan for your project.
- *Who will you be writing for?* There are different rules/guides for different audiences. Are you writing for a clinical project committee? A research review board? A course faculty member? Who else are you writing this proposal for? Spend time considering your

various audiences and the implications of these different groups for the project proposal expectations and requirements.

- *What tools/techniques are available?* It's important to know about the available resources for increasing efficiency as well as effectiveness. In addition to the broad proposal guidelines outlined in this text, often specific guidelines are available to assist you in crafting clinical project proposals with specific purposes such as coursework or grant funding. To begin, what specific guidelines are available to guide you in crafting the proposal? Are there templates to guide completion? Is there a time frame for proposal completion? Is there a page limit? From a practical perspective, drafting an early table of contents that outlines all the required components is a useful strategy.
- *What are your qualifications?* What education and experiences have prepared you to propose and write up a specific project proposal? Or to use specific methods? Or to even study the proposed concept? Just as an athlete would not undertake a major athletic event without preparing, it is important that you also have or gain the background, education, and skills to propose and complete the clinical project.
- *Are there practical concerns or ethical issues in a particular topic?* As part of clinical projects, both practical and ethical issues and concerns must be addressed. For example, if you would like to learn more about patient function in specific home settings for your elderly population, what practical issues must be addressed in making home visits? What potential ethical issues might need to be addressed if you wanted to take videos of the patient in the home for analysis?
- *Will you be able to carry out the project you are proposing?* Striving for a project that is not too big and not too small can be a challenge when you first begin your project planning. Mentor and peer review can provide benefits of additional perspectives to help deal with finding the proper balance.

STRATEGIES TO KEEP THE SCHOLARLY
WRITING PLAN MOVING FORWARD

Motivation for doing clinical projects is often high while thinking and planning, but students anecdotally share that actually writing the proposal can be a challenge. Considering the proposal from the positive frame of thinking through the "big picture" and keeping the end in mind can be a form of motivation. Writing the proposal with the project triangle in mind, with the goal to ultimately getting the purpose, methods, and outcomes in alignment, will provide the foundation for a well-organized clinical project that helps improve clinical practice.

Big-Picture Tools and Problem-Solving Strategies

All scholarly writers need a good starting point and tools to keep moving their writing forward. Starting with a good clinical problem (Chapter 3) can help motivate and keep you moving forward. For example, taking an area of interest or a concern/challenge (that you believe will truly improve patient care) and then studying it with a quick assessment of related concepts/issues through a concept map can be helpful. Concept maps have the benefit of visualizing multiple related concepts or issues that may be related to or influencing the problem.

Problem solving fits with concept mapping as a brainstorming tool to identify possible antecedents to the problem and to identify particular patterns that emerge. Visualize or push your thinking first to the big picture of the problem and then to the full project.

Other tools to visualize big-picture issues include diagramming and outlining approaches. These also have the benefit of exposing the big picture of potential aggravating or causative factors. As noted, using a fishbone-type diagram can help identify important factors or components influencing problems. Additional approaches such as problem-solving question prompts can help one brainstorm. Brainstorming itself, or rapidly generating ideas relevant to your topic, is valuable as you begin a project. This includes asking the right questions such as: What if? and I wonder? Paragraphs highlighting sample tools are presented here.

Mind Mapping or Concepts Mapping

Developing concept maps provides a beginning reflective activity. Maps help you think about key points surrounding a particular problem and provide potential options to consider before making your case as to why this is an important problem. When completed following a literature review, these can also help you determine what evidence is there (or needs to be gained) to make your case. Moving beyond basic related concept identification, further diagramming can help identify possible interrelations (such as spider diagrams or extended Venn diagrams). Asking who-, what-, when-, and where-type questions can also help diagram out the topic/plan.

Planning Arrows

With similarities to concept maps, planning arrows help organize thinking on specific topics. Sometimes called a fishbone diagram, this tool provides direction in naming potential challenges impacting one problem area. Using a systems perspective, planning arrows remind you to consider structure-and-process issues that may be impacting particular outcomes.

Reflective Writing Strategies

Reflection is a key tool to not only begin writing but also to keep writing progressing. Reflection, scholarly dialogue, and scholarly writing/projects are tools that can also help cope with clinical change and help to cement learning and further plans. Reflecting and generating further questions are also consistent strategies used by the qualitative researcher, suggesting questions as you study and encouraging new thoughts/issues.

The One-Page Early Reflection

One approach to using reflection as you begin a project is to start by writing about why you are choosing a particular topic. This would include, for example, the interests that led you to this topic. If you have several topics in mind, complete a one-page reflective paper on each topic that addresses the following: What do I already know/think/feel about this topic? And what questions do I still have? These reflections help address why these topics/projects are important to you and which will be the most interesting and provide the greatest clinical value to you and others. Other reflective writing techniques can be helpful at various points in the project, with examples following.

Ongoing Journaling/Reflection

Ongoing journaling spending even 20 minutes a day on a project can promote success. It is important just to establish the routine/habit and get something project related on paper. For a jump start, combine this habit with already established rituals, such as a morning cup of coffee.

- *The concept of structured questions/writing prompts* to guide written reflections adds more direction to journaling. This practice promotes tracking what you already know about your project and helps identify areas needing further attention or further questions (Wolcott, 2008). Consider using the reflective questions incorporated throughout this text as writing prompts to get you going and keep you going.

- *Free writing* leads to learning more about your thoughts and subsequently organizing those thoughts. Free writing involves letting words flow without concern for spelling edits or others' eyes. The goal is to simply get content/thoughts on paper. You then have something to edit and share with colleagues so that others will understand.

Documenting Tools to Further the Writing Plan

Especially when writing a large project over time, there are benefits to record-keeping tools to help track factual information, resources, and project decisions.

Outlining is described as an art and offers the following benefits: firming up thinking, organizing materials, and gaining a logical step-by-step method. It also helps identify gaps or excesses and can promote unity and emphasis on key points and provides a visual impression (Savers, 2011). Others use a broad outline format, focusing only on broad concepts that will guide, rather than focusing on numbered details.

Decision trails or decision logs are factual records. This means keeping an annotated list of your work as you go along. This provides a scholarly record of what actually has been done and also can help you remember why you made the decisions you did. These tools are further discussed in later chapters.

BENEFITS OF SEEKING WRITING REVIEWS

Self-Editing

You will want to start with self-editing, a process in which you read and re-read your written work to make sure it clearly states your intended ideas. As the number of times you read your own words increases, it's easy to start gliding over them too quickly to edit effectively, so it's helpful to read your work out loud to slow yourself down and to hear different inflections that can be read into your wording and punctuation choices. Also putting the paper aside and revisiting after several days provides opportunity for clearer self-evaluations of the writing.

Peer and Mentor Reviews

Peer and mentor reviews are also good editing approaches. Peer review includes reviewing, interpreting, and communicating evaluative information to a peer. This can be a formal or informal process that helps nurses provide feedback to peers based on specific criteria. Typically this is an interactive process and involves use of specified guidelines or rubrics based on criteria to guide the feedback. Remember that a combination of positive and constructive feedback is most helpful—exclusively positive feedback feels good and exclusively negative feedback is destructive, and neither contributes to excellence; hence, be sure to provide a balance between positive and constructive comments.

Seeking formal reviews from mentors is also key. Points to consider include the following.

- Be proactive in seeking/gaining feedback on your writing trouble spots.
- If you note trouble spots in your writing, re-work what you have written. If you cannot give up any of your works, open a file named "Extra" to copy and paste information for potential future use.
- Seek out writing centers at schools or from private resources to guide you if you are experiencing problems conveying your thoughts clearly. Writing centers provide guidance, not on your content, but on your process for organizing and conveying written information.

SUMMARY

Although much of this chapter focuses on approaches to writing up a clinical project, it is also about tools that make writing a part of clinical scholarship. Writing is a way to name and package what you are doing or planning to do. A writing plan can lead to successful proposals that then lead to successful clinical projects. The self-directed writer becomes adept at organizing time, place, and space. There are various tools to help the clinician writer stay motivated and organized to move forward with writing tasks for clinical projects.

TIPS FOR GETTING STARTED

- Stay focused on the project topic.
- Get something on paper.
- Gain writing experience.

- Address the beginnings–middles–endings formula like "speech" class to help outline a proposal. In addition to the main "middle" message, the introduction summarizes what you will tell the reader and why it is important. An effective conclusion then summarizes what has been accomplished.
- Use time-management strategies like tracking the time allotted and used for clinical proposal writing.
- Remember your decision trail and journaling for recording your ideas/decisions.

NEXT CHAPTER UP

How do you shape the problem statement? You have ideas, a plan for writing; now it is time to focus on organizing information on one specific problem area. Moving from the messy "problem" to the real issue and fine-tuned problem statement is a next step.

LEARNING ACTIVITIES

Writing Prompts

Writing prompts provide a way to reflect and get some ideas on paper. Use these prompts to brainstorm possibilities.

1. I want to study more about this topic because . . .
2. My background will help in the following ways . . .
3. Areas I still need to gain knowledge/skill in include . . .
4. A beginning plan for gaining these skills includes . . .

CHECKLIST AND GOAL SETTING FOR GENERATING A WRITING PLAN

To which of the following can you check "yes"? Which of the following needs to be further addressed?

Are you:

1. Writing regularly with reasonable ease?
2. Focusing on what you are to be writing?
3. Avoiding distractions of excess reading/other?
4. Using peers/advisors when needed?

5. Using an efficient writing process?
6. Moving forward?

Do you:

1. Have a project/writing timetable?
2. Feel good about your writing process?
3. Have a process that's working for you?
4. Have a steady writing pace that feels reasonable?
5. Have a pace consistent with your calendar for finishing the project (Bolker, 1998)?

3

Writing a Good Clinical Problem and Placing the Clinical Problem in Context

REFLECTIVE QUESTIONS

In Chapter 2 you learned about tips for organizing your writing. Now the focus is on determining and naming the problem that will be the subject of your writing, putting that problem in context, and creating a written problem statement. The following reflective questions organize learning for this chapter. Which of the following do you have the most comfort with?

- Identifying areas of clinical practice that you find most interesting, problematic, alarming, or confusing?
- Isolating problematic areas of clinical practice that could be changed to improve patient care?
- Clarifying the problem name and its description/definition?
- Explaining the significance of finding a solution to the problem?

FROM AREA OF CONCERN TO PROBLEM STATEMENT

This chapter is about taking an area of concern and turning it into a clearly named problem. Broadly described, clinical problems relate to topics that provide clinicians and clinical leaders opportunities to improve patient care. A problem refers to a situation that needs a solution. Naming a problem can lead to evaluating and packaging new approaches that promote safe clinical care delivery and products for clinical education and leadership. Good problems have good practical implications, are well delineated, and promote personal and career interests (Krathwohl & Smith, 2005). The final problem statement sets the stage for generating the project purpose and methods for completing the work.

Where Do Areas of Concern or Problems Come From?

As you know, clinical problems come in all shapes and sizes. As a good reflective clinician, you probably have many "problem" ideas already. Current specialty "issues" that may serve as project ideas are often described via professional nursing meetings, funding sources, and specialty newsletters. It is also important to look around and see what current challenges exist in your clinical setting. What is happening, or not happening, that impacts safe, quality care? Sometimes this problem is approached from a gap analysis, the space between "what is and what should be." In other words, what still needs to happen related to the area of concern?

Clinical problems can be unique or common. Some will have relevance to specific areas of a unique practice setting. Others might have relevance to diverse settings or broad health promotion issues of populations. Sample brainstorming options to help you generate specific clinical problem areas include:

1. Wondering about clinical unit problems from recent practice experiences. Is there a better way? Wondering if what worked well in one setting might be considered in your current setting? For example, wondering whether a specific evidence-based communication protocol would enhance your own unit communication?

2. Having conversations with others and reviewing competence in clinical practice settings. Are staff meeting competencies matched to current standards? Or implementing practices according to standards for a new/revised technology such as insulin pumps? What practice concerns do your colleagues identify?

3. Thinking about ways to improve staff education on clinical topics, documentation standards, or interprofessional practices. For example, are current pain-management protocols expanded to include holistic healing approaches?

4. Considering clinical needs for quality improvement. Asking for example if best policies and practices are being used in select areas such as peripherally inserted central catheter (PICC) line practices?

In this chapter, as part of thinking about a problem area to spend time on and to use as the focus of your clinical project, several "problem" aspects are considered. For example, how do you focus a problem for study? How do you know it is an important problem, and how do you know that you are choosing a reasonable problem to pursue as a scholarly clinical project?

FOCUSING THE PROBLEM: BRINGING IDEAS TO SHAPE

The goal is to take a broad problem area, or area of concern, and turn it first into a focused problem and then a specific problem statement, moving from a general problem to a specific problem. Areas of concern are different from focused problems. What turns an area of concern into a focused problem? For example, as a clinical leader in long-term care, naming the "group dining setting" for frail elders as a "mess" may accurately state an area of concern, but it lacks direction for improving the elders' dining situation. Moving from a broad fuzzy area of concern to a specific problem(s) is one of the first parts of project development. What do you specifically mean by your "problem"? In this group dining situation, are there staffing issues? Lack of adaptive equipment? Poor environmental arrangements?

Again, early project work involves making sure you are identifying and naming a problem that can be focused. Once the problem is named, then you will go on to writing a problem statement and then following that, the project purpose statement. Concurrent with this writing process, you will be searching the literature. The literature review adds to finding out what is known and not known about this clinical problem. It addresses if and/or how others have considered or addressed this or similar problems.

The literature related to your area of concern not only helps with naming and describing the problem but will also help as you move forward with a project plan. The literature review gives you direction for moving forward and identifying whether the problem is evidence rich or limited in evidence. It addresses whether the evidence you are finding can help with further solution planning. For example, as you have conversations with other professionals about the group dining room in your long-term-care setting, use problem-solving models and review the literature to identify various issues that lead to problems within this setting.

Sample approaches to gain conversation ideas on topics of interest or problem areas include:

- Start reading broadly and then become more specialized
- Review tables of contents for sample naming of problems or approaches to a problem

- Review textbooks on a topic of interest to identify broad select challenges
- Seek synthesis articles first and then follow up with specific studies
- Contact experts in the field

FOCUSING THE PROBLEM: NARROWING THE TOPIC

Once you begin describing the problem, there is almost always benefit to narrowing your topic to be very specific for your project. This helps in naming the problem more clearly, reviewing the literature, and then projecting further clinical study plans. In essence you are seeking movement from that fuzzy problem or "mess" to a clear problem statement and potential plan. Narrowing or funneling, seeing the change from a large global problem to a more concrete, detailed problem, also makes it seem more like a do-able clinical project topic. A funneling approach, starting broadly and then narrowing, is approached by continuing to ask, Would a more narrow focus help name and evaluate the topic while still providing the important information?

For example, related to the group dining topic in long-term care, thoughts might proceed as follows: the group dining room situation is a "mess" and needs to be better; then, which patient groups are having the most challenges? Then, what does the literature say about working with these patient groups? Or perhaps you will determine another pathway to narrow, such as staffing issues seem to be problematic; then, which staff seem to have the most challenges helping patients or who could provide more help? What does the literature say about staffing issues, both in general and in long-term care dining settings?

Using another example, even if you have determined there is a unit need for palliative care education, you still have a very broad statement with limited specifics about what that means. Moving forward you would take this broad topic and determine specific educational areas for your focus. Looking at this broad topic, sample approaches might be to narrow it to areas such as pain or symptom management or family involvement in care. These concepts could be further explored and narrowed to the many areas, all within this broad problem, that could help improve patient care. When a range of options is identified, it will be easier to focus on the specific needs for unit staff education and to further focus a project plan. As soon as you have narrowed the focus, it will be easier to move forward in naming and packaging what you will do in your clinical project.

How best to continue to narrow or clarify a clinical problem? As noted in the palliative care education example, most problems start broad and then need to be narrowed to a much more specific, direct focus. How else might you narrow or bring your problem/concern into focus? As you consider your broad fuzzy problem, consider knowledge from theory, evidence-based practice, and research in naming specific concerns. Further chapters in this text provide direction in these areas.

Additional Brainstorming Tools

When you have identified a problem or broad area of concern, consider whether any of the additional brainstorming tools could be used to further focus the problem. Brainstorming tools can help first identify big-picture issues (as noted above, the top of the funnel), but they can also help in narrowing to a more specific aspect of a broad problem. These tools can also help place the problem in context (determining what the problem issue is and what the surrounding factors are). Additional strategies to help focus the problem and to consider problem context include:

- Fishbone diagrams, which help name and organize the potential factors that can be impacting a problem (as discussed in an earlier chapter)
- Concept maps or concentric-circle diagrams (as discussed in an earlier chapter)
- Addressing the who, what, why, where, and when related to a particular problem

FOCUSING THE PROBLEM: CLARIFYING THE PROBLEM NAME AND DESCRIPTION

Why is clarifying the problem name important? Basically you have to make sure that your project team and future readers know what you mean by the use of the selected term. You will have to confirm that others agree with this terminology or that your use of the term is consistent with how others (e.g., in the literature) are using it. Even if your project becomes a broad exploratory approach to learn more about the problem, you will still need broad descriptors of the concept you are studying. Depending on the problem you choose to study, describing/defining is often considered similar to or a basic step of concept analysis discussed in Chapter 6. Resources such as the work of Walker and Avant (2011) provide further details.

For example, if you are concerned about the problem of increasing incidents of delirium in health care settings, first you will need to define and describe what is meant by delirium. How does the best evidence or literature define and use the term? If you wish to pursue a project that includes palliative care education, you will need to further define what the term "palliative care" means, for example, differentiating or identifying similarities and differences to the concept of hospice. Note also that you have indicated the concept of education as a part of the problem solution. For a scholarly project you need to further describe what the concept of education will mean. The basic question to address is: What are you naming your concepts and how are you defining your concepts for study? That includes naming what concepts are as well as clarifying what they are not.

FOCUSING THE PROBLEM: DESCRIBING CONTEXT AND SETTING BOUNDARIES

What makes the problem context and problem boundaries important considerations? Part of naming and defining the problem includes putting the chosen problem in a selected setting or identifying the problem boundaries for purposes of the project. Context is the broad setting, and the boundaries establish what is included in and excluded from that context.

Naming the context or setting boundaries helps you and your reader understand what you are doing as well as what are you not doing related to this problem. Stating, for example, that "x" will be included in the project but "y" will not helps identify the boundaries of the problem you plan to study and frames the problem to more clearly identify where it stops and starts. This also helps limit the extraneous issues and extraneous data, making the project more clear and manageable. For example, which of the following provides more focus:

- The context/boundaries for this project are all elderly patients in this hospital with risk factors for delirium.
- The context/boundaries for this project are patients with a dementia diagnosis on a surgical unit who are at risk for delirium.

Note that the second statement above provides more direction. The intent is to further narrow and determine what is most important and most feasible or practical to include in the project (Leedy & Omrod, 2013). In simple terms, this means putting a frame or circle around the topic/problem/issue you are addressing and then describing the surrounding factors.

WHAT MAKES THIS A GOOD AND IMPORTANT PROBLEM TO STUDY

What makes your problem an important one to study? Why is this problem significant to others? Does it matter or make a contribution to practice?

Does it address a practical, clinical concern? Use the following additional questions to guide your thinking during problem-statement development and write-up.

1. Is the problem of current interest? Is it topical?
2. Is the problem likely to continue into the future?
3. Will more information about the problem have practical or theoretical application?
4. How large is the population affected by the problem?
5. How would study of this problem lead to improving the problem or extend existing knowledge about the problem?
6. Would clinical project findings potentially lead to some useful change in best practice?
7. Is there current research or evidence that supports the need for further study of this problem? (Adapted from Robinson, 2010)

INTRODUCING THE PROBLEM IN THE PROPOSAL

Problem Significance

Discussion of the problem significance provides the rationale for why you are taking on the project. Much of the challenge is articulating the specific clinical problems and challenges so that others understand. Here you introduce and make the case for the importance of the problem you want to address. This includes describing the background of the problem. Addressing broad issues includes providing a brief summary of current knowledge of the problem being addressed in broad populations or organizations. Addressing local issues includes describing the nature and severity of the specific local problem or system dysfunction to be addressed. Finally, summarize a specific statement of the problem to be addressed in the project. This problem statement then leads to identifying the project purpose, setting the stage for determining best methods to guide the project.

Fine-Tuning the Problem Statement

The problem statement serves to describe the important issues or conditions that exist in leading to the proposed project. An effective problem statement names the extent of the problem and supporting evidence, identifies factors contributing to the situation, and notes current gaps in addressing the problem (Coley & Scheinberg, 2007).

Although the background of the problem is described in multiple paragraphs, a specific statement comprised of several sentences that summarizes the problem is beneficial to you in clearly naming the problem as well as communicating its significance to others. This statement clearly identifies your area of concern as a specific problem and provides the focused name of an issue you plan to study in some way. It names what the problem is and clarifies what it is not. The problem statement is part of the first section of the proposal. It follows your discussion and introduces the reader to your problem. After reading your summary of the problem, ask yourself:

- Can I clearly answer the question: "What is the problem"?
- Is the scope appropriately limited with a balance of completeness and conciseness?
- Can I state why this problem is important and why it is worthy of a project?
- Does the problem summary place the specific problem in the context of the larger world? Does it describe the problem as important and interesting?
- Does the problem statement set the stage for a reasonable project to follow?

Common Challenges With Problem Statements

After fine-tuning your problem statement, it should clearly and concisely identify the clinical problem your clinical project will address, as well as its context. Review your problem statement and make sure it doesn't fall prone to any of the following mistakes:

- It is not clearly stated or is vague and lost in general discussion.
- Components that contribute to the problem are not well identified or addressed.
- Limited or weak data are presented in support of the problem (and not logically organized).
- There is limited interest or need for study of the suggested problem.
- The problem is not framed in an adequate context (Leedy & Omrod, 2013).

Peer-Review Activity

Again, recall the value of peer/mentor review. Discussing the problem statement (and other project components) with others can help you improve your work. As you review the following problem statements, determine whether the problem statement is well focused. You want it to be specific enough to provide direction for your project. If you were completing a peer review for a colleague, do the two problem statement summaries below provide beginning project direction? What details would you recommend adding to either statement?

- Standardized electronic health record (EHR) documentation helps meet clinical, legal, and payment requirements. EHRs improve communication and efficiency in gaining patient information and documenting patient encounters. In reviewing the literature, no studies were found specific to staff challenges and attitudes toward EHR documentation. A problem exists in helping staff best accept and prepare to use EHRs.
- College students are a unique population. College is an important transition time, and the health behaviors students choose in college often set the stage for lifetime health behaviors. A problem exists in helping students gain motivation and action toward improved health behaviors.

Using the Title to Help Convey the Project

The project title is the most-read component of the project. Clearly naming the problem and the title can work together to promote project clarity. This includes naming what the problem is and what it is not. For example, if you are naming a problem related to staff development for older adult care, there is a lot of variation with the following names, "dealing with the frail elderly" versus "promoting wellness for older adults." These names provide two very different pathways. Both can be of value, but early decisions as to the project's direction will better guide the project work. The correct name contributes to or sets the path for a good project.

Incorporating the problem into the project title is only one component. When your project purpose and methods take shape, they will influence the title as well. As your problem statement progresses and you move into the purpose-statement phase, you will begin to think about the overarching title of your project. Being able to name what you are doing can help you stay with your intent. Don't over-promise what your proposed project can accomplish. Peer review could include asking others what they think your title conveys.

Project Triangle

It is not too early to start getting points of the project triangle to align. After the problem is clearly named and described, use of the project triangle comes in. The problem statement will then lead to developing your project purpose. This will be important as you develop your outcomes and methods. For example, in a project to learn about staff issues with a new EHR system, a very simple project triangle might include: purpose = understand staff concerns and satisfaction with the new EHR system, methods = staff complete survey on concerns and satisfaction questions, outcome = evidence for any needed staff development.

SUMMARY

Clinical problems with relevance for advanced clinical projects abound. The problem statement sets the stage or describes the status of a current situation that needs to be addressed. It serves as the background for project purpose statements. It helps if the problem statement emerges from strong personal interests and promotes academic and career interests. Concepts from this chapter suggest direction in identifying important problems and focusing them for further study.

NEXT CHAPTER UP

You now have a problem statement clearly crafted. This problem statement serves as a guide as you next return to the literature on the topic. With a concise and accurate problem statement in hand, you are ready to delve more deeply into the literature on your focused problem area.

LEARNING ACTIVITIES

Your Story Related to Your Topic of Interest

One way to begin developing a problem of interest is to write about it from a personal perspective. What is your story related to your topic of interest? Why is it important to you? What do you hope to accomplish? As you identify a problem of concern, write a few paragraphs about what it means to you and why it is important to you. This reflection can help focus the problem and provide an opportunity for you and faculty to communicate. For a specific problem that you have in mind:

1. What makes this problem important?
2. Why does it matter? Are there important patient concerns? Staff concerns?
3. What potential contributions could be made from further studying or developing this project?
4. What surrounding clinical issues seem to work well with this problem?
5. What could be working better?

Further Reflective-Writing Prompts

1. I am choosing this topic because . . .
2. It is important I do this project because . . .
3. Challenges in taking on this topic include . . .
4. Early findings from the literature review suggest. . . .

To-Do List

- Find three key articles that most help you make your case and move your project forward for the problem you think you would like to pursue.
- Identify and confirm a specific topic of concern that can be addressed by the clinical project.
- Write an introduction that presents the importance of your clinical problem and what is known about it. End the initial section of your proposal with a clear, one- to two-sentence problem statement that clarifies what the problem is and why it is important.

Readiness to Move On . . .

1. Have you started a literature review related to your problem?
2. Have you tried to think about the problem from all sides and perspectives?
3. Have you considered the pros and cons for addressing this problem?
4. Have you gained expert advice on strategies and challenges for your planned approach to the problem?

4

Into the Literature: Gaining Best Evidence and Relevant Literature

REFLECTIVE QUESTIONS

The following reflective questions organize learning for this chapter. Which of the following do you have the most comfort with?

- What makes a good systematic literature review?
- What does the concept of "information literacy" mean to you and why is this relevant to your project proposal?
- What are the best strategies for completing a systematic literature review?
- What does it mean to complete a reference matrix?

WHAT MAKES A GOOD LITERATURE REVIEW?

A good literature review is one that is systematically documented, synthesized, and situated in the context of the professional literature. Your literature review can help you narrow your practice concern in order to best name the problem you are studying. The literature also provides ideas about how much your problem area has been studied. Coping with the vast quantities of literature available involves more than an informal literature review. The review for your project should be systematic, covering important aspects of the topic, and be representative of the work that has been done. Also a systematic literature review can be combined with an annotated bibliography or review matrix to help organize information. For example, if you are seeking best evidence on caring for new patients with stroke on a rehab unit, what is the best evidence available about that care in the literature? Your systematic review and reference matrix will provide the basis for an evidence-based synthesis of this literature.

THE REVIEW OF LITERATURE AS THE BASIS FOR FURTHER PROPOSAL WORK

Gaining awareness of existing knowledge regarding practice is critical to a good clinical project proposal, and this requires systematic approaches to the literature review. The formal systematic literature review, as previously noted, should be reviewed simultaneously with the development of your problem statement and purpose statement. A systematic review of the literature during these two steps helps to narrow the problem, gain project direction, and establish the need for the project.

As you write your problem statement, the review of literature familiarizes you with the best evidence that currently exists specific to your chosen problem. The review of literature also helps describe the context for the specified problem and patient population. It should also remain ongoing so that the references you describe in your project truly reflect the rapidly changing evidence on your specified subject. This implies that the literature should be consistently updated throughout the clinical project duration.

A thorough review of literature also establishes you as an expert in the area and enables you to demonstrate your command of the literature, best evidence, and gaps in knowledge related to your topic and its context. This means you know the key authors writing in your topic area, you know the existing knowledge base on the topic, and you are able to identify the strengths and weaknesses of the evidence related to your clinical problem.

Finally, gaining and synthesizing the evidence are part of the scholarship of advanced clinical practice. Your contribution to clinical scholarship is best if situated within past and present knowledge in the area. Identifying gaps in the topic can help make the case for your additional project work. Box 4.1 provides a summary of additional ways the literature will be useful in your project proposal.

BOX 4.1

Multiple Approaches for Using the Literature in Your Proposal

Although much of this chapter addresses literature review as part of the detailed critique of literature on your specific topic, the literature also supports other sections of the proposal. Examples follow.

Section 1: Problem Statement and Introduction

As you introduce and make the case for the importance of the clinical problem you want to address, this will include describing the background of the problem and documenting its significance. The literature and other best evidence can be used to help describe both local and broad contexts for the problem. As you note local issues, describe the nature and severity of the specific local problem or system dysfunction to be addressed. Furthermore, relate this to broad national or global issues related to the problem.

Section 2: Literature Review and Critique

This section includes a focus on the systematic literature review you are completing. Describe your literature-review methods, including at minimum databases searched, years searched, and inclusion/exclusion criteria. Also, as described in Chapter 5, you will be synthesizing your findings. This will include organizing and summarizing your literature review, often by themes; then summarizing the strengths and weaknesses of the literature related to your problem of interest.

Section 3: Your Project Methods

In this section you will talk specifically about the literature you have reviewed on the methods your project will use. As you critique other studies, you can gain ideas for your own project methods.

Further Literature Use in Your Completed Project

Once your project is completed, you will also return to the literature and place your project findings in context of the literature. This includes identifying similarities and differences in findings related to your project and others reported in the literature.

BEGINNING THE LITERATURE REVIEW

A good literature review begins with information literacy. Information literacy means knowing when information is needed, identifying the type of information needed, finding and evaluating the information, and organizing and using the information to address the problem (American Library Association, 2009). Additional concepts relevant to information literacy include synthesis of accumulated information, clear communication of search results, and consideration of social issues and ethical aspects regarding information dissemination (Jacobs, Rosenfeld, & Haber, 2003). Simply stated, information literacy means you have to locate, read, analyze, and organize the current state of the evidence or science (Galvan, 2006). For example, in better understanding eating issues experienced by patients with Parkinson's disease, you will have a responsibility to locate and critique relevant literature as well as to responsibly report a synthesis of this information so that it is useful to others.

Today's technologically oriented world both eases and complicates this process because of both the quantity of available information and the rapidly changing nature of that information. Although on the one hand advanced technologies have made searches much easier to conduct than during pretechnology days, on the other hand, the same technologies have made searching much more complex because of increased options and the sheer volume of information available.

Although informal reviews have their place, the scholarly, advanced clinical project requires a formal review. You cannot claim you conducted a thorough review of the literature without providing the details of your search so that others can evaluate your thoroughness. Therefore, the care with which you conduct the review of literature takes on greater meaning and must be clearly documented. The quality of your review serves as the foundation for your advanced clinical project; if you miss relevant literature, you may repeat work that has already been completed or fail to establish a legitimate case for the significance of your project.

Although it is easy to find information in today's world, it is more challenging to find good information. The review must yield information that can legitimately serve as the basis for your project and withstand scrutiny from the scientific community. Use of a hierarchy of evidence (Polit & Beck, 2012) enables you to identify the strengths/weaknesses of information, and thereby establish its credibility, or lack thereof. Part of being scholarly is addressing the quality of the information you are using so that you address the credibility of your sources.

FORMAL REVIEWS OF THE LITERATURE: THE PROCESS OVERVIEW

The goal of a formal review of the literature is to search and obtain evidence, review and critique the evidence, and generate an evidence summary. These components support generation of a synthesis or state-of-the-science summary of your findings as well as a decision trail documenting the process. This chapter discusses obtaining and critiquing the literature. Synthesizing the literature will be addressed in the next chapter.

The first step in the literature review is to gather relevant information with a broad general search of the literature. As you progress in naming and refining your clinical problem, your advanced clinical project will become more focused, as will your continued review of the literature. It is vitally important to recognize the review of literature as an ongoing process, rather than a discrete step that is conducted and marked off your to-do list, because as your project progresses you will learn of added concepts and have more precise information to search. Also the literature can change rapidly, and you must always be working with the most up-to-date information and current context possible.

THE LITERATURE SEARCH: OBTAINING EVIDENCE

There is an art to searching for and obtaining appropriate literature, and this process involves multiple phases. In early phases of the literature review, the goal is to fine-tune your problem statement. As previously discussed, the problem statement provides a succinct statement of the issue or topic of interest and provides the necessary information on which to further refine your literature search. Early in the process you will need to make important decisions regarding the search. These decisions relate to databases, key words, inclusion/exclusion criteria, and practical/methodological screens.

Databases

An initial decision will be which databases to search. In early search phases, go beyond the nursing literature to identify how other disciplines are using your topic-of-interest concepts. At minimum, begin the search using PubMed, CINAHL, ERIC, and Google Scholar. Keep track of the "search terms" you use as you search the literature. Consider whether you need to supplement your electronic database search with additional strategies, such as reviews of professional journal tables of contents or reviews of the reference lists on previously found articles, to address your project purpose. This is especially useful in early stages to identify how others are naming and framing selected problems. Also keep a decision trail outlining your process as further discussed below.

Key Words

In addition to determining the databases to search, key words you will enter into the database to search need to be determined. This will begin with key words that come to mind related to this concept from your personal experiences; also reviews of relevant articles and the key words they note will help establish the initial boundaries of your topic. Also consider which search terms are preprogramed into the specific databases you are using as a means of organizing content in that particular system.

Inclusion/Exclusion Criteria

Next comes adding further structure to your review. How will you further structure your search if your search provides excessive or irrelevant resources? One benefit of problem statements and purpose statements is that they help identify and clarify the project's scope and limits. For example, if you are reviewing best evidence on pain-management protocols, you will likely need to clarify what patient groups this includes. As chronic pain management with dementia patients has different context than pain management for those with acute back pain injuries, inclusion and exclusion criteria noting these issues for the search are needed. Inclusion criteria indicate what will be included in the search, and exclusion criteria mean what will be excluded. These concepts are similar to "practical screens" as further discussed in the next section. Note that in initial stages of the review it may be useful to consider the similarities and differences in how related topics are covered.

Practical/Methodological Screens

Both practical and methodological screens help frame the topic. "Practical screen" refers to naming the types of references to be included. These practical-screen criteria could include, for example, the disciplines' databases to be considered, publication years to include, and language options (most often limited to English-language articles only). Identifying terms that you will be studying, as well as those terms you are not studying, helps avoid comparing "apples to oranges." "Methodological screens" refer to those clarifying the level of study or quality of evidence you are seeking. For example, your review might note that only articles that are based on data would be included. Fink (2010) provides further background reading and direction in using practical and methodological screens, as well as article critiques.

If you are new to the process, a successful literature search will be facilitated by working with a more experienced searcher, such as a librarian and/or a content expert. The best searches are conducted by people who know both the mechanics of literature searches and the content area.

CHALLENGES/FACILITATORS IN GAINING THE EVIDENCE

Various challenges may arise when searching the literature. These relate to lack of literature, issues of accessing quality references, and tracking the literature obtained.

What if You Can't Find Research/Literature Evidence?

Sometimes even the most systematic search yields no results, and this may cause you to make one of two decisions. The first possibility is that no evidence currently exists, in which case your advanced clinical project will need to address this situation. The other possibility is that evidence exists, but, to date, you have failed to access it. Perhaps you have not yet used the key terms or database that will lead to the information you need. Optional approaches in this case include reaching out to databases from other disciplines, stepping back and using different or broader search terms, or seeking expert consultation.

Another possibility is that the evidence that exists is not found in the literature, per se. In this case, it is important to consider what other types of documents and resources could be counted as evidence. For example, national health care professional organizations often serve as clearinghouses and resources for the best evidence. Professional organization websites, such as the Alzheimer's Association or the American Diabetes Association, typically provide extensive evidence-based resources that supplement the more traditional review of the literature.

What if Accessing or Obtaining the Evidence Is Problematic?

Another potential obstacle is that, although you find reference titles that sound good, the articles are not available to you locally or, if available, do not provide a high-quality discussion or evidence on the topic. In completing a systematic review, you then have responsibility to note these types of issues.

How Can a Decision Trail Help Track the Search?

In addition to saving your literature searches, be sure to keep a decision trail that enables you to reconstruct the decisions made during the search and the rationale that guided the search process. A decision trail is an objective accounting of the processes used in completing the search. This provides a type of accountability in the steps you have taken to ensure a comprehensive search.

For example, if your interest is in nursing ethics, consider the search process. How many articles do you find after searching the word "ethics"? What did you find when you then search the combined words "ethical decisions"? Is there a difference when you use "ethical decision making"? How many articles do you find for this search phrase and how many of those were relevant to your topic? Do you refine the search further and, if so, using what new key words and why? Now consider the fact that these questions are answered in a very short time period and the quantity of findings and subsequent decisions grows exponentially. As noted, you will determine a system by which you keep track of this information.

This concept is additionally extended to what databases were chosen for the search and what rationale led to these decisions. A beginning strategy is to save every search you make, such that you have a record of the terms and search engines used, as well as the search results. Additional notes in the form of a decision trail will remind you at a later time why you made the decisions reflected in your searches. Again, these documents will be important as you summarize in your proposal the systematic approach you used in reviewing the literature. Again, the basic tip is not to trust your memory but to document your process.

The following are components that should be included in summarizing the process used for your systematic review. Clearly describe each of the following in your decision trail:

- Search terms and search strategies used. Include a summary of search trail/phrases that led you to the articles reviewed.
- Inclusion/exclusion criteria (i.e., specific criteria for this review such as literature time frames to consider and populations to consider).

- Practical/methodological screens considered.
- The databases that you searched.

READING AND CRITIQUING THE EVIDENCE

Once your search is over and you've obtained articles, your activities shift from information seeking to information reading and critiquing. The term "reading process" can be misleading in that it involves much more than just reading. Recall the vast amounts of information available today. The quantity of information requires methods by which to organize, store, and evaluate the merit (or lack thereof) of information obtained in an efficient manner.

To Help in Reading

Use active reading to narrow the field. First preview the article and then use questions to address further in reading (i.e., questions about studies/findings: who, what, how big/little, where/how outcomes were gained?). Also as you read, consider the following approaches:

- Identify common themes in the literature.
- Clarify interesting points or irritating questions.
- Organize/confirm thoughts on a topic.

To Help in Critiquing Individual Articles/Evidence

There are various hierarchies of evidence established to differentiate the quality of evidence. It's important to identify which hierarchy you're using and to provide sound rationale for that decision, and then to use that hierarchy consistently throughout your advanced clinical project. For example, Polit and Beck (2012) use a seven-level hierarchy ranging from level I (systematic review of randomized controlled studies [RCTs]) to level VII (opinions of authorities and/or expert committees). The Cochrane Collaboration (http://www.cochrane-handbook.org) specifies four levels of evidence, ranging from the highest level I (randomized trial evidence) to the lowest of case series and case reports. Their system uses additional evaluative factors, such as limitations in the design, inconsistencies in results, and wide confidence intervals, as reasons to decrease the quality level of the evidence.

Although hierarchies vary, the fundamentals of their ranking systems are consistent. For example, both systems previously noted would place a synthesis article that organizes the findings of similar research studies higher on the hierarchy than a single case study. The basic premise is that "reading" does not just mean reading; it also means evaluating and critiquing the quality of what you are reading.

ORGANIZING THE LITERATURE REVIEW

As evidence is identified, obtained, read, and critiqued, you will need a mechanism by which to organize all of your information. There are a number of options, and you will likely need to use more than one of them:

Archiving and Cataloging

You will need an organized and competent system for keeping track of the evidence you find. At the very least this should consist of an electronic system, either a commercial software package (EndNote, OneNote) or your own computer-based system (e.g., in Excel). These resources provide the opportunity to easily record the references you find and highlight details of the content therein. Further work is needed in the form of a reference matrix.

Reference Matrix

The more robust approach to organizing is the reference matrix or bibliography table. The matrix or bibliography table helps you to organize, gain an overview, and then be able to summarize in rapid fashion what you have gained (Galvan, 2006). This matrix or table serves several purposes. First, it helps to organize the growing number of individual articles and evidence you find on your advanced clinical project topic. Second, it provides a beginning synthesis of the literature as a whole, which will be your next step in the process. The matrix also provides the context for how your project can help extend the knowledge/literature on this topic. Paragraphs summarizing and synthesizing the findings emerging from your matrix are then easily organized in your project proposal. The matrix itself may become an appendix in your proposal. Finally, the matrix serves as a quick snapshot summary of the evidence and an easy communication tool for your team members.

Reference Matrix Format

The matrix is generally a table format with a row for each piece of evidence and various columns for different information about each piece of evidence. All matrices will include standard information, such as the full article citation, but the remaining columns will be guided by the needs of your particular advanced clinical project. You may include, for example, the level of evidence in one column, the methods used in another, the population, the setting, strengths, and weaknesses. Although you are free to create your own headings for columns in your matrix/table, you will have to include key components. For example, columns or components for the table that are often important to your project include key terms/concepts definitions, research study methods, critique of the study, and summary of study findings. At minimum, a summary table, listing strengths and weaknesses of each article, is needed in your archiving/cataloguing system. Box 4.2 provides an example of headings for a literature matrix.

BOX 4.2

Sample Matrix Headings

Citation	Participants/ Setting	Purpose, Background	Methods/ Design and Limitations	Findings/ Summary Strengths/ Weakness	Applicability to Own Research

The matrix/table can be created using various tools, but common tools include Microsoft Word and Microsoft Excel. Sometimes a strategy that begins with Excel and then copies and pastes to Word provides advantages. Although this matrix may appear to be an extra step at this point in your project, in the long run it will make the critique and synthesis of the literature much easier. Also recall that the literature is constantly being updated. You will have to consider this a work in progress as you find additional resources to add.

Final Touches to the Matrix

As you finalize your matrix and prepare to write up your findings from the literature, you may ask, is this a reasonable matrix? Guidelines to consider include addressing the following questions:

- How much literature is enough? Have you started with a broad approach to the topic and then narrowed your topic adequately to gain the detail of a specific component?
- Have you searched at least one database beyond traditional discipline literature?
- Are you getting saturation from the references you are finding (no really new ideas are emerging from articles)?
- Have you considered whether there are classic references to include (those included in everyone else's reference list that can provide some historical perspective)?

Documenting Sources

Documenting sources and reference format are considered as a part of written scholarly communication. American Psychological Association (APA) format is the tool used in the nursing profession to ensure that scholarly references are provided in an accessible format. Getting a citation correct initially saves lots of problems down the road; hence, plan to summarize article notes (in your reference matrix) in a format that can be cited.

SUMMARY

Completing a systematic literature review as part of your clinical project is a key component of clinical scholarship. Additionally, part of being scholarly is addressing the quality of the information you are using and using credible resources. The systematic literature review and matrix provide a beginning place to discuss the credibility of resources/references.

NEXT CHAPTER UP

Chapter 5 is about synthesizing the literature review. After completing your reference matrix, the next step is to synthesize this literature into a document that summarizes the state of the literature about your problem.

This provides you an opportunity to identify strengths and gaps in the literature on your topic. Your conclusions to the literature review will help connect the problem statement to your project purpose statement.

LEARNING ACTIVITIES

To-Do List

1. Work on your decision trail for your systematic literature review. As you progress on your systematic literature review, confirm you are on track with each of the following:
   - Search terms and strategies described, including specific databases.
   - Summary of search trail/phrases that led you to include the articles reviewed.
   - Inclusion/exclusion criteria noted (i.e., specific criteria for this review such as literature time frames to consider, populations to consider).
   - Practical/methodological screens considered.
2. Work on your reference matrix. Choose categories to organize that help you best capture information for your synthesis. Include for example:
   - Citation
   - Participants/setting
   - Purpose, background
   - Methods/design
   - Findings
   - Summary strengths/weakness
   - Applicability to your own project

Reflection Paper With Project Question

Select a concept related to your project interests and generate a question to guide your literature review. For example:

- What is the evidence for using "concept maps" as a teaching/learning strategy for patients with diabetes?
- What are the best practices for using "debriefing" as part of simulations for staff development?
- What are the best practices for using "group projects" in online courses for staff development?

5

Synthesizing Best Evidence and Literature Review

REFLECTIVE QUESTIONS

The following reflective questions organize learning for this chapter. Which of the following do you have the most comfort with?

- What does it mean to synthesize the literature? Why is this important?
- Why is the evidence/literature synthesis important to your project?
- What does it mean to identify themes from the literature review? Why is this important?

Synthesizing is a step that is additive to the literature review. Synthesis is about describing similarities and differences in articles and drawing conclusions about the literature as a whole, rather than each article individually. It provides the big picture of what research is available (and not available) and its overall quality. It incorporates the critique of studies reviewed, but it also adds integration or synthesis of the results. It involves identifying strengths and weaknesses of the systematic literature review.

For example, your colleague has an interest in complementary health approaches for pain management. He reviewed the literature on yoga as strategy to support pain management but was surprised at the variety of ways yoga was defined and the variety of pain-related diagnoses that yoga was used with. Even after creating his matrix of studies on yoga for pain management, he realized that more analysis and summary of the big picture of the research/evidence on the topic was required. Because of the variation in concept definitions and populations, it was important that he identify similarities and differences so that he could be sure he was comparing similar approaches or at least clarifying the differences in the types of yoga and the variability in the populations in which it was used. This was done in addition to determining the strengths of the evidence for his matrix studies.

Just as your hypothetical colleague found in the above example, even after creating your matrix of individual articles, you will need to further analyze and synthesize the big picture of the literature to better understand and convey your topic to others. You need to use the evidence to frame your chosen problem and to identify solutions/strategies that others have used. Your proposal synthesis will include a summary and analysis of findings from the literature search.

Although the introductory section of your proposal uses literature to describe your problem and related issues, the specific literature-review section addresses the more detailed systematic review of the literature. Now you take each article or piece of evidence placed in the matrix (Chapter 4) and, after comparing and contrasting that evidence, draw conclusions about the findings and the quality of those overall findings. This chapter addresses synthesizing or crafting the big picture of the literature review.

CREATING THE LITERATURE SYNTHESIS

Synthesizing the literature involves moving from a critique of individual articles to describing and commenting on findings as a whole from the literature and other evidence sources. Synthesizing is noted as additive to summaries, takes the project to the next level, and creates information sharing in a new way via the pulled-together resources (Galvan, 2006). Synthesizing involves:

- Taking separate articles and blending them into a synthesis of the topic to help you better understand the state of the evidence related to your problem
- Showing the coherent flow or evidence of the specific literature reviewed, including description of the important concepts/themes and how they fit together
- Sharing a meaningful interpretation, synthesis, and report on the combined literature findings

Your synthesis will provide a description of the current body of knowledge in your clinical area. It can help make a case of the need for, or for the merits of, your proposed clinical project. Presenting this synthesis in a logical way with these steps also makes the review more easily accessible to others.

Begin by Reviewing Your Reference Matrix

The matrix has helped you organize information and now helps with easy retrieval and flexible use of your review (Garrard, 2010). To begin the written literature synthesis, you will return to your completed reference matrix. Recall that in your matrix, you have summarized and critiqued the individual studies. Now you are describing/analyzing what you found as a whole.

Begin by reviewing and critiquing your reference matrix and making sure that it is finalized and ready for synthesis. Check to see whether the following components are complete in your matrix.

- References are appropriate and useful and come from respected publications.
- Your findings are clearly identified from research and other evidence-based sources.
- The summary of each article is relevant, clear, and accurate.
- Good critique of reported studies is provided.
- Unique or interesting points from each article are noted.

Move From Individual Article Description to Critique/Synthesis of Matrix Articles

Typically the first draft of a project literature review tends to be a compilation of descriptive paragraphs about each individual study. This is problematic in that the draft is missing the study critique and the synthesis of the findings. For example, if your literature review is similar to the following hypothetical project, then you have not yet synthesized the literature:

- Author 1 conducted a correlational study on stress with 50 participants and found frequent comments about crisis and specific relationships to anxiety . . .
- Author 2's descriptive study looked at anxiety. She interviewed 15 participants and found that subjects related anxiety to stress . . .
- Author 3 conducted a qualitative study with 10 participants experiencing crisis and found themes of stress and anxiety . . . .

If, in contrast, you have focused more on the following format, then you are on the right track to creating a literature synthesis from these three articles:

> Several studies have found that there is a relationship among anxiety, stress, and crisis (Author 1; Author 2; & Author 3). Although two of the studies were qualitative in nature and used appropriately small samples, all three support the nature of the concept relationships and need for further study.

Further Consider the Matrix Findings

Now that you have considered steps to synthesize several articles, you are ready to move forward to a larger synthesis of your full reference matrix. As noted previously, you will synthesize your matrix via summaries of content and study methods. Synthesizing the literature does not mean just a recounting of the references via random listing. It focuses on a summary or synthesis of the big picture of the references reviewed. When summarizing and synthesizing your big-picture review of the literature, additional questions and phrases that may help you synthesize your literature review (i.e., as you look for strengths, weaknesses, or gaps in current evidence) will include the following:

1. What summary statements can you make about the level of evidence from the various studies/reports and the findings associated with them?
2. How much variation was there and how was your concept defined/considered/delivered across the studies/reports?
3. How much variation was there in the outcome(s) studied across the studies/reports?
4. What findings are supported by more than one study/report?
5. What findings are supported by just one study, but are compelling? Why are they compelling?
6. What findings are inconsistent across the studies/reports?
7. What findings are outright contradictory across the studies/reports?
8. What further questions do you still think need to be addressed? (Fink, 2009; Garrard, 2010).

ORGANIZE THE SYNTHESIS

Organize the Synthesis Summary Statements

Approaches to organizing and synthesizing the literature review include grouping the important project concepts/themes, variations in concept definitions or populations, and variation in methods quality. These findings from the literature can then be used as headings to help guide the reader through the literature-review section.

- *Important themes*: This involves identifying each of the main concepts/themes involved and then providing a descriptor or definition from the literature. If there are differences in how the term is described, note this so as to avoid comparing "apples to oranges." For example, if "support group" is your topic of interest, are you reviewing online or face-to-face groups (or both)? If both, you will organize findings so that this is reflected. Then summarize the strengths of the literature and then describe gaps or areas with limited research. If additional themes emerge from your references, the approach (noted above) can be completed for each theme. Summarize the commonalities and the differences for studies within each theme. Add a final summary noting the overall themes and strengths/weaknesses of the literature in describing your problem of interest. Points to include in your discussion include the following:
- *Variations in concept definitions or populations*: In the introductory example, the definitions of yoga and the populations using yoga were quite diverse. Multiple studies were noted using varied concept definitions and treatment definitions that could not be easily used for outcome comparisons. Organizing your synthesis by grouping varied definitions can be a useful approach. This will be an important point to convey in your synthesis summary, noting that the current literature makes comparisons and generalizations challenging.
- *Variation in methods quality*: Also consider methodological themes informing the quality of the findings as a way to organize the synthesis. For example, randomized controlled studies with large samples provide very strong evidence compared with small descriptive studies. Critique your reference matrix and summarize what was found. Questions that you used in critiquing your matrix findings can assist with this as well.

Note that Appendix 5.A provides an example of a literature-review final summary. The themes summarized are broad communication issues, barriers to effective communication, improving telephone communication in long-term care (LTC), and potential liability issues. In your full summary of the literature review, you will include article summaries and citations.

PREWRITING THE SYNTHESIS

Create an outline for the literature synthesis. Outlining your synthesis includes the following points.

1. Write an introductory statement to the literature review reminding the reader of the review's purpose and explaining the significance of the concepts to be described.
2. Provide evidence of current, comprehensive, and synthesized literature review with a clear description of literature-review methods and project components/processes.
3. Once key themes or categories are identified, then outline these with specific references. Some find it helpful to begin write-ups with a PowerPoint summary. The small spaces or bullets force an economy of words and focus on what is most important in the synthesis.
4. By concept or theme, in a few sentences, summarize the major approach and findings of each reference/study reviewed (including appropriate citation of the resource).
5. At the end of each major concept/theme discussion, summarize the key points supported. This includes a written summary statement at the end of the literature review explaining the knowledge available, as well as the gaps in the literature. You can then finish by discussing conclusions/implications that are a logical next step with the literature.

MOVING TO THE FINISHED LITERATURE SYNTHESIS

Write the Introductory Section to the Literature Synthesis

Briefly remind the reader why this literature review is important and its purpose (to enhance/support your project). Include for the readers an introduction that provides a map of what will be covered in the literature review (Galvan, 2006). Also state the limits to the review or what will not be covered. For example, this review addresses only adult patients and not children. Recall your purpose for the literature synthesis. Remind the reader of what you mean by the terms and why this is an important topic.

Include the Systematic Literature-Review Methods

Begin the literature-review section with a summary of the methods used for your systematic review. This must include the primary search strategies, including at a minimum: the databases searched, key words or phrases included, and any time boundaries for the literature. To document your review methods, go back to your decision trail and list the databases and the key phrases searched.

Include Overview and Summary Statements

Recall the benefits of introductory and summary statements. A feature of this literature synthesis is to communicate to others what you have learned. Therefore, one priority is to make this section especially easy for your readers to follow. This is facilitated by beginning each section with an overview of what will be presented and then summarizing at the end of each section exactly what was presented. Although it may seem redundant to you, it helps the reader who is not so intimately familiar with your project stay on track.

FINISHING-UP CHECKLIST FOR LITERATURE SYNTHESIS

The following points provide guidance in synthesizing the literature and will help you confirm you are on the right track in reviewing and synthesizing the literature specific to your chosen problem. Did you:

- Discuss implications of literature findings specifically related to your project purpose?
- Address relevant theory?
- Use headings to provide visual signals for the reader?
- Summarize at the end of each section; describing the major themes related to your problem and project purpose, and discuss how the themes are related?
- Minimize paraphrasing and minimize direct quotes? Excess quotes slow the reader down, so only include the very few that are most pertinent or necessary.
- Read and review for logical presentation and coherence?

RELATING THE LITERATURE SYNTHESIS TO
THE CONCEPT OF "TRANSLATING" EVIDENCE

Does synthesizing the literature relate to or include translating the literature? In a time of complex clinical problems, nurses are needed to identify approaches that help patients manage their care with approaches that come from an evidence base. Nurses can translate that evidence, which basically requires synthesizing that evidence into meaningful useful protocols and then implementing and evaluating those protocols for utility.

To translate requires first synthesizing what is available as evidence. For example, with chronic pain/relaxation protocols, that means search first for strong studies with tight experimental design. Additional data (if extensive experimental data are not available) can be gleaned from descriptive data and practitioner reports. After gaining the best evidence base, this can be organized into protocol format for further testing. Further testing of evidence can be done by implementing and evaluating the protocol.

This chapter has particular relevance for clinical projects that involve evidence summaries. For example, with chronic pain management, one of the top disabling medical problems, there are a variety of medication and nonmedication approaches available. A sample project purpose might relate to what non–drug-related approaches are useful to people with chronic pain. For example, what does the evidence say about relaxation and chronic pain? Further addressed might be how do nurses implement protocols as coaches?

SUMMARY

Synthesizing the literature can provide a critical analysis and summary of the existing literature in your clinical area. In developing this synthesis of best evidence on your topic, you describe the current state of the evidence/science. Through identification of the strengths/weaknesses of the research and evidence in your problem area, you provide the rationale for your project. You describe the significance of your proposed clinical project proposal and how it will extend the knowledge/literature on this topic. Your conclusions about the literature serve to frame the problem you intend to address and the approach you propose. A good synthesis allows you to move your proposal forward in creating a succinct problem statement and generating a project purpose statement.

NEXT CHAPTER UP

Theories and conceptual models provide excellent tools to help organize clinical projects. Chapter 6 addresses frameworks to guide your project.

LEARNING ACTIVITIES

To-Do List

1. Critique your reference matrix. Make sure it is ready to move to synthesis format. Can you affirm you have provided each of the following?
   - Clear description of literature-review methods and project components/processes?
   - Evidence of current, comprehensive literature review documented via your decision trail?
2. Begin the synthesis of your literature review. As you seek themes from your reference matrix, have you addressed each of the following points?
   - Considered how much variation there was in how your concept was defined/considered/delivered across the studies/reports?
   - Addressed how much variation there was in the outcome(s) studied across the studies/reports?
   - Considered what findings were supported by more than one study/report?
   - Considered findings that were inconsistent across the studies/reports?
   - Thought about findings that were unique, but compelling?
   - Considered summary statements you can make about the level of evidence from the various studies/reports and the findings associated with them?
   - Thought about further questions that you still think need to be addressed?

APPENDIX 5.A: LONG-TERM CARE COMMUNICATION: SUMMARY OF LITERATURE REVIEW*

Methods

A systematic literature review was conducted. Databases searched include PubMed, CINAHL, and Google Scholar. The key words are *nursing home, long-term care, communication, telephone medicine, quality improvement,* and *nurse–physician relations.* The literature review included research studies and articles from 1997 through 2011 and was limited to health care–related

---

* Note that the paragraphs in this section are not a full literature review, but rather a summary of a literature review for the project described in Appendix D.

articles. Articles were excluded if they were not related to health care professionals or communication. References from key articles were also retrieved and reviewed. The review revealed that one group of researchers from Duke Medical Center did extensive work on this topic. Author searches were done on each member of this group. The following themes organized the literature review: overview of communication issues, barriers to effective communication, improving telephone communication in long-term care (LTC), and liability issues.

Review Summary

Many studies have been done looking specifically at telephone communication between LTC nurses and physicians. These studies addressed barriers to communication, importance of communication, and methods to improve communication. The studies also described how structured communication can improve the quality of care or how poor communication can lead to error and liability for the provider and facility. Many of these studies have addressed after-hours phone calls in the setting of Veterans Administration nursing homes and/or physician training programs. These facilities have physicians on-site during daytime hours. The literature does not address phone calls to physicians during daytime business hours. For LTC facilities and physicians without daytime on-site coverage, multiple phone calls are disruptive to the office staff and, unless it is an emergency, the LTC nurse often waits for long periods for a return of call. Many of the studies evaluated interventions aimed at improving physician skills with telephone communication. Few studies focused on interventions to improve nursing skills with telephone communication. No research looked at RN and licensed practical nurse (LPN) roles in communicating with the physician even though the LPN is rapidly becoming the primary nurse caregiver in the LTC setting. Several studies demonstrated that relatively short clinical educational programs were effective in teaching both RNs and physicians how to better communicate clinical information to other professionals.

6

Framing the Advanced Clinical Project With Relevant Clinical Frameworks

REFLECTIVE QUESTIONS

The following reflective questions organize learning for this chapter. Which of the following do you have the most comfort with?

- What is a theory or conceptual framework?
- What does it mean to frame a project?
- Why is this important?
- What is an appropriate framework to use?

Theories and frameworks serve as an organizing resource to guide clinical projects or organize plans for change. The right framework provides organization for proposal writing as well. In Chapters 4 and 5, you learned about finding evidence and synthesizing the relevant literature for your project. That literature helped to focus your problem statement, while at the same time providing its broader context. In this chapter, you will concentrate on placing your clinical project into an appropriate and useful framework.

The need for a framework to guide projects is universal. Consider the prospect of trying to improve quality health care in the United States without any direction at all—how would you know where to start and what to do? The U.S. Department of Health and Human Services has released a framework to guide this work in its National Strategy for Quality Improvement in Health

Care (National Quality Strategy [NQS]). Based on the latest evidence and input from a broad range of stakeholders, the NQS identifies three aims for health care (better care, affordable care, and healthy people and communities). Further guidance is provided via six priorities, including reducing harm associated with health care, engaging people and families in their own care, promoting good communication and coordination of care, promoting effective prevention and treatments, engaging communities to promote health-related best practices, and making quality care affordable. Although still a daunting task, the NQS framework provides broad direction on how to go about improving health care (National Strategy for Quality Improvement in Health Care, 2011).

THE VALUE OF THEORIES AND FRAMEWORKS

For the purposes of this text, the terms "theory," "framework," and "conceptual models" are used interchangeably. That is not to deny the important historical conversation about distinctions in terminology that has transpired, but what is relevant here is that theories, frameworks, and/or conceptual frameworks can all serve the required purpose of guiding the clinical project. A clinical project of very broad scope may benefit most from a broad, systems theory or conceptual framework, whereas a project of very limited scope would benefit from a situation-specific theory. Again the terms "theory," "conceptual framework," "conceptual model," and "framework" are used interchangeably in this text to refer to the guiding framework for your clinical project.

WHAT IT MEANS TO FRAME A PROJECT: THE PROJECT TRIANGLE

Recall the triangle, with the points identified as the purpose, methods, and outcomes. Drawing on the aspect of conceptual models as drawings or depictions of a theory, the triangle itself represents a theoretical framework for the clinical project, as it connects those points with three straight lines. The lines provide the boundaries for the clinical project and enclose the concepts involved, and they provide the overall consistency needed for the project. As long as the three lines remain in the shape of a triangle, the framework provides structure and holds the project together in a consistent and cohesive whole. If inconsistency or misdirection occurs within the project, then the framework becomes askew with three disjointed lines rather than the desired triangle. In this case, it's time to, literally, realign by pulling back and reviewing the overall triangular structure of your project before moving forward again with the proper direction.

THE IMPORTANCE OF FRAMEWORKS

Frameworks serve several important purposes in clinical projects, but those purposes are so fundamental that the use of frameworks is often unconscious and their role unnoticed. Although theoretical frameworks are invariably employed, the absence of their explicit use threatens the recognition of frameworks as a necessary part of professional nursing. Students complete clinical projects as they move into leadership positions in nursing, and they assume responsibility for helping the profession recognize the dependence of their practice on theoretical frameworks. More specific purposes of theoretical frameworks as they apply to clinical projects are that they provide the necessary elements described in the text that follows.

Boundaries

Frameworks/theories are abstractions of reality and, as such, they represent real situations in nursing. The framework used to guide a clinical project should provide a foundation for the project and establish the extent of its scope. A broad theory may be appropriately chosen to guide a very wide-ranging clinical project, whereas a middle range theory might more appropriately guide a more limited topic such as quality of life or patient education. In either case, the framework establishes the boundaries of the project.

Structure and Relationships

The framework also provides structure within the established boundaries by identifying the concepts included in the project and, depending on the framework, how they are related to one another. In a patient teaching/learning project, the appropriate framework must include both patients and teaching/learning, and it may also define the relationship between teaching/learning and patients, such that the education may vary depending on the age of the patient or learning might increase with greater amounts of teaching time. Although both children and adult patients may benefit from active participation in the education, adults may need recognition of past life experiences that very young children do not. The theory may also suggest that repeating content is important for both children and adults.

Concept Definitions

The concepts used within a framework are defined according to their meaning in the framework's context. Part of your work in choosing a framework involves critiquing the model's concepts and how they are defined. This is particularly important in naming your outcomes of interest and how they will be evaluated in your project. Some frameworks may define teaching as teacher centered, whereas others define it as learner centered. Neither is necessarily right or wrong, but they are different, and whichever framework is used must fit the theoretical definition that you are using in your clinical project. It is also imperative that the instrument used to measure teaching in your clinical project defines the concept of teaching consistently with your definition.

Efficiency

Because the framework provides boundaries and structure, and perhaps even direction, it increases efficiency in the project. For example, the framework provides common definitions for the concepts so that confusion about terminology is eliminated. Similarly, the framework identifies the necessary concepts, so time is not wasted on extraneous concepts or variables that do not apply. If confusion sets in, return to the framework to determine whether this or that concept requires time and attention.

Organization

With the borders, structure, and direction provided, frameworks may offer several other practical benefits. The framework may provide a reasonable format for presenting the project's review of literature, for example, or suggest a means by which to organize a questionnaire and/or provide substantive content for the questions asked.

Consistency

Although theories do provide the previously stated benefits, they also provide a means of tying those individual benefits together into a consistent, cohesive, and comprehensive whole. The framework ensures that the boundaries of the project are consistent with the concepts involved in the project, which are consistent with the literature that is reviewed and the means by which the concepts are defined, measured, and analyzed. The framework is the means to consistency among the project purpose, the methods, and the outcomes.

SELECTING AN APPROPRIATE FRAMEWORK

The most appropriate framework is the one that best fits your clinical project and that is determined by evaluating potential frameworks for a good match. In fact, "critiquing theory is a necessary part of the process when a scholar is selecting a theory for some disciplinary work" (McEwen & Wills, 2011, p. 119). Nursing has a strong tradition of dialogue about the appropriate criteria on which to critique theories (Chinn & Kramer, 2011; McEwen & Wills, 2011; Meleis, 2012; Peterson & Bredow, 2013). For the purposes of guiding clinical projects, the following are suggested criteria for evaluating the appropriateness of potential frameworks.

Scope

One criterion for choosing an appropriate framework is how broad or narrow the focus of the framework is and how well that fits the scope of your clinical project. If the project focuses on patient education, then a broad theory is too general and the focus of the project is lost; conversely, a framework with too narrow a focus will potentially omit vital concepts. Consider focusing on the clinical project through a camera lens. If the wide-angle focus is too broad, the patient being taught may hardly be identifiable in the picture; conversely, if the wide angle is too narrow, then the patient may be cut out of the picture altogether. The framework must provide the proper scope, such that both the patient and teacher are in the picture with enough clarity to see and study them.

Context

In addition to providing scope, the framework provides the context of the project, and that context must be consistent with the project. If the project has to do with teaching dressing changes at home, then the theory must address that residential context, as teaching a patient to do dressing changes in the hospital where supplies are abundant and time is protected is far different from doing so at home where the supply of gauze has run out and there are competing demands from work and family. So the framework must account for a context that is consistent with the project.

Logical

The framework used for the project must be logical and make sense. This does not require in-depth testing, but may be a simple matter of whether the framework makes sense in your own experience. For example, does the teaching theory suggest that the most beneficial relationship between patient and teacher is that they ignore each other? If so, the theory does not make sense. But if the framework suggests that interaction between the patient and teacher is desirable, then it does make sense. Choose only theories that make sense and are logical.

Assumptions

Frameworks are generally based on assumptions. This is neither good nor bad, but true. So it is imperative that potential theories be evaluated for the assumptions made, and whether those assumptions are consistent with the clinical project. For example, some education theories may assume that learners are ready and want to learn, whereas others do not. So if the clinical project aims to address the education of newly diagnosed and resistant teen-aged diabetics who are generally in denial, then the educational theory that assumes the learner is ready to learn would not be appropriate.

Useful

There is no reason to consider a framework that is not useful to your work. Therefore, the theory must at least include the concepts that are inherent in the clinical project, as well as pertinent information about how those concepts are related. Consider, for example, the project of building a house. Before the actual building project begins, a picture of the house is drawn. That picture (model, framework) provides the scope of the building project, outlines the structure and its boundaries, defines the relationships among the various rooms in the house, and serves as the basis for the building project. This picture is a very useful prerequisite for the project of actually building the house and serves to keep the project on course throughout the building process. So it is with your clinical project and its framework.

Simple

Although vitally important, the framework itself is not the topic of the project, so it should not be complicated or demand undue time and effort to explain. Rather, the framework should be easy to understand

and not detract from the time and focus spent on the project itself. Although the student should consider the preceding criteria, there are several aspects of choosing a framework that are not of practical relevance and therefore do not need to be given a great deal of attention. For example, choose the framework that best fits your project and do not spend time worrying about whether it is a nursing theory or borrowed from another field. Many important theories that guide patient education arise from other fields, such as education and psychology, and their practical contributions should not be ignored just because they were not developed within the nursing profession. Similarly, do not worry if your project requires the use of multiple theories. For example, in the situation of patient education, it may be important to use not only a cognitive developmental theory but also a behavioral learning theory. Similarly do not be concerned if you find several frameworks, any of which could serve as useful and appropriate frameworks for your project. There may not be just one, absolutely right, framework; rather, any one of several frameworks might serve your purpose.

SAMPLE FRAMEWORKS

There are lots of theories and frameworks that could serve as potential project frameworks. That means there is likely to be at least one framework that will be helpful to your project, but the task of finding the most appropriate framework for the project might be daunting. Remember that the framework is not the focus of the project; its job is to quietly support and guide your project. If there is one obvious framework, great! If not, there may be several that would be equally good. Commonly used frameworks include (but are not limited to) the areas of nursing, physiology, teaching/learning, developmental psychology, systems, management, leadership, social psychology, and quality improvement. There are generally numerous options of theories/frameworks, and a good first step is to brainstorm known theoretical frameworks that might work in the project. Also conduct a cursory review of the literature to see what other possible frameworks might fit. The objective is not to find the most complicated and obscure theoretical framework but to find a fairly comprehensive list of potential frameworks for your project. Box 6.1 provides suggestions for several different project topics. Once you have reviewed the table, consider your own project topic and identify at least three potential frameworks to guide your work.

Although there are numerous frameworks that can be generally considered for a project, it is the match between the project and the framework that is important. If multiple potential frameworks emerge, the

BOX 6.1

Sample Project Topics and Theories

Project Topic	Potential Theoretical Frameworks
Patient education	Behavioral learning theories Cognitive Cognitive development Constructivism Adult learning
Change the care delivery system	Systems Change Quality improvement Transformational leadership Theory of reasoned action
Improve treatment of patient pain	Selye's general adaptation syndrome Gate control theory Opponent process theory Motivation-decision model
Determining the child's role in care	Psychoanalytic child development Cognitive child development Behavioral child development Social child development
Implementing a new program on smoking cessation	Health belief model Self-efficacy Motivational theories
Research utilization and evidence-based practice	Iowa Model ACE Star Model
Quality improvement	NQS Plan–Do–Study–Act Model

next step is to determine which framework is the most appropriate for the project. For example, if the project purpose is to implement a change in care delivery, then potential theories might include systems, change, quality improvement, transformational leadership, or theory of reasoned action. But as your purpose statement is refined and becomes more focused, you will identify additional details that determine which theory best fits the specific purpose and scope of your project. For example, if the purpose evolves into focusing on the role of the nurse in implementing system changes, then perhaps the theory that best matches that purpose will be transformational leadership. Now reflect on the list of three potential frameworks you created moments ago and critique each framework for its fit with the refined purpose statement for your specific project.

Once you have brainstormed potential theoretical frameworks and then narrowed the list to those that truly fit your project in terms of scope and focus, you may find that you still have several choices. If so, one useful approach is to pick the best-known theory, as it will serve to support and facilitate the project without demanding undue time or attention. Examples of many clinical projects can be found in Doctor of Nursing Practice capstone projects. For example, the Doctor of Nursing Practice website provides numerous examples (www.doctorsofnursingpractice .org/studentprojects.php). The following clinical projects are listed on the basis of having explicitly identified the framework for their projects:

- Brewer's (2009) project *Pediatric Nurses' Attitudes and Knowledge Regarding the Provision of Breastfeeding Support in a Pediatric Medical Center* used the theory of reasoned action.
- Evangelista-Hoffman's (2009) project *Emergency Department (ED) Sepsis Care: Application of the Iowa Model of Evidence Based Practice (EBP)* used the Iowa Model of evidence-based practice.
- Filaskovsky's (2007) project *Effect of an Intervention to Increase Knowledge of the Danger of Delay in Seeking Treatment for Chest Pain* used Leventhal's self-regulation model of illness behavior.
- Halon's (2011) project *Improving Depression Screening, Diagnosis, and Treatment in a Diverse Urban University Health Service* used the Plan–Do–Study–Act (quality improvement) framework.
- Hayne's (2011) project *Using Problem Based Learning to Analyze Health Policy* used a problem-based learning framework.
- Peterson's (2009) project *Using the Transtheoretical Model in Primary Care Weight Management: Tipping the Decisional Balance Scale for Exercise* used the transtheoretical model.
- Sanchez's (2010) project *Implementation of Diabetes Self-Management Education Using Shared Medical Appointments in Primary Care for Adults* used a chronic care model.
- Santucci's (2010) project *A System Change: Expansion of Primary and Secondary HIV Prevention in a Marginalized Community* synthesized a model using constructs from the health belief model and the Community Readiness Model.

FINAL THOUGHTS

Whether explicit or implicit, frameworks are invariably used to guide clinical projects. For example, in the project *What Nurses Need to Know About Sleep Apnea* (Morton, 2012), the theories are not explicitly identified, but clearly both physiological and learning frameworks were used. Another project, *Applying Lean and Six Sigma to Your Dermatology Practice* (Rice & Haycraft, 2012), explicitly describes how the frameworks of Lean and Six Sigma can be used in practice. As clinical students move on to leadership roles, it's important that they not only use theoretical frameworks to guide their own work, but also guide the profession by helping other nurses consciously recognize the theoretical foundations of their practice.

NEXT CHAPTER UP

Now that you have the purpose of your project identified, and that purpose is framed within a theory/conceptual model, you are ready to identify the outcomes for your clinical project. Outcomes are one of the three key elements of the project triangle and are extremely important as they provide the focus for your entire clinical project. The outcomes need to be based on the clinical problem you want to address and will provide the foundation for the project's purpose statement and methods.

LEARNING ACTIVITIES

To-Do List

1. Scan the literature and your past textbooks. Identify and list at least three potential theories/frameworks that could address your project's purpose statement.
2. Referring to the three potential theories found, and using the criteria provided in this chapter, critique each for its potential use as a framework for your project. Pay particular attention to the concepts and how they are defined. What direction does this framework provide you?
3. Identify the most appropriate framework and justify your decision.

Reflective Prompts

Reflections and questions to guide your thinking about how to frame your project include:

1. Is the framework appropriate for this project?
2. Does the framework fit the scope and purpose of the project?
3. Does the framework provide useful guidance regarding the scope of the project?

4. Are all of the key elements of the purpose statement represented in the framework?
5. Is the framework simple in nature and easy to understand?
6. How will the clinical project benefit from using the framework?

Activity

Using guidelines from the National Agenda for Quality Improvement in Health Care (2011), which models or theories can you think of that could help you further your review of the literature or plan for an evidence-based project?

- Make care safer by reducing harm caused in the delivery of care.
- Ensure that each person and family is engaged as partners in their care.
- Promote effective communication and coordination of care.
- Promote the most effective prevention and treatment practices for the leading causes of mortality, starting with cardiovascular disease.
- Work with communities to promote wide use of best practices to enable healthy living.
- Make quality care more affordable for individuals, families, employers, and governments by developing and spreading new health care delivery models.

7

Addressing Outcomes Evaluation in the Advanced Clinical Project Proposal

REFLECTIVE QUESTIONS

The following reflective questions organize learning for this chapter. Which of the following do you have the most comfort with?

- Considering rationale for seeking varied project outcomes?
- Considering approaches to gaining project outcomes?
- Considering benefits/challenges to seeking selected project outcomes?
- Beginning the plan for project outcomes?

Outcomes are important expected considerations in documenting quality patient care and are important in clinical projects. They can be dependent variables in research projects or staff competencies in educational projects. In the clinical setting, positive outcomes are often related to accountability and serve as indicators of success. So it is important to select reasonable outcomes for which you know you can gain reasonable data. Too often specific project outcomes are not fully considered. Outcomes evaluation, which is often an afterthought, is really such a key part of the proposal that it receives its own separate chapter in this book. This chapter focuses on the outcomes that you will be seeking, as part of your choice of project methods and tools. It includes detailing the "outcomes" point on the project triangle and beginning to consider evaluation of those outcomes.

CONSIDERING PROJECT OUTCOMES/EXPECTATIONS

A majority of clinical projects include evaluation components such as those projects using continuous quality improvement or new protocol or program evaluations. These clinical projects identify expected outcomes, just as a hypothesis identifies expected outcomes in a research study. They project what is to happen, similar to a research hypothesis stating expectations. Individual case studies have evaluation components as well.

As suggested by these various approaches to considering the evaluation concept, the term is used in different ways depending on the context. In a research project, the dependent variables are identified as the outcome variable, that is, what is being measured/observed. If you're planning a staff development or teaching project, then seeking student competency on a subject or behavior may be an appropriate outcome. If your project involves administrative outcomes on a unit, the outcomes might include staff retention or increased patient satisfaction scores. A public health/ population project might identify outcomes such as improved symptom or chronic disease management outcomes, decreased medications, or decreased falls.

As noted, outcome evaluation is a broad topic and covers many variables and perspectives. In this chapter, common considerations are addressed. In addition to the project triangle, discussion includes outcomes as part of a systems model and principles that guide good outcomes evaluation.

OUTCOMES EVALUATION AND THE PROJECT TRIANGLE

Writing a project proposal incorporates many components, with the project triangle key in helping align these components. Part of this process is making outcome choices fit with data-collection methods. As you recall the triangle in which the purpose statement, methods, and outcomes represent the three angles that need to mesh, a key feature of evaluation and outcomes is keeping these three components (purpose, methods, and outcomes) aligned with one another. For example, education departments want to document that their programs have a purpose to impact staff, patients, and organizational outcomes. Evaluation choices at the end of an educational session include outcomes such as knowledge, behaviors like patient care/documentation, and values. Evaluation methods then need to be identified to document these outcomes.

Outcomes evaluation is described as addressing impacts of a program or intervention and can be considered from short-, medium-, and long-term perspectives (McNamara, n.d.). Outcomes help provide the project focus and show whether a difference has been made because of the project.

When talking about outcomes, parts to consider include: naming the outcome and then determining how best to define and evaluate that outcome. This relates to the definition of concepts and how to operationalize or measure the concept. Conceptual definitions were identified in Chapter 6 as components of the conceptual framework. In this chapter you will begin to think about how that theoretical concept is defined and will be measured in your clinical project. This means you will first be naming the selected outcome concepts and then defining what they mean. For example, if you hope to influence pain outcomes, will this mean a physical measures score or a patient self-rating on a checklist?

SYSTEMS MODELS AND OUTCOMES

This is an important time in health care to be addressing clinical outcomes and considering those outcomes as part of a systems framework. For example, as nurses you are working in very complex health care, educational, and community settings. A systems model, focusing on structure–process–outcomes, is very helpful in managing and evaluating the multiple components of such complex settings. Part of evaluation is naming what you do (i.e., identify our product) and describing what you do (the process) and what structure/resources you use to gain these outcomes. This means considering outcomes as part of a systems framework. Outcomes in isolation, without considering structure and process, have limited value.

For example, if your project consists of seeking improved staff educational outcomes, knowing the specific outcomes you are going for helps you focus the structure/process for the educational project as well. Seeking the right structure and process can help address what some of the issues may be for the program's successes or failures. This is an example of the strategy of backward design. It is part of the broad systems approach to evaluation (structure, process, and outcomes). Backward design provides the opportunity to first identify the outcomes that you are seeking and then work backward to project design.

Just as in the pain-management example, outcomes provide the project focus. The specific outcomes sought relate to the project's purpose and methods. Working backwards from desired outcomes helps name what the product is and knowing what you are hoping to achieve. The outcomes statement helps name the big picture of the project and why it's being sought. It typically helps to work backward from an outcomes statement to gain direction for what tools to use.

OUTCOMES VARY BY PROJECT TARGETS

All outcomes should relate to your purpose statement, but, beyond that, there are numerous choices. For example, population outcomes can be broad or specific. They can address global "improve quality" topics or specify unique population outcomes. For example, health promotion evaluation protocols are very different for an adolescent than for an older adult. If your project involves nursing assistants in long-term care, a focus on outcomes typically includes determination of an improved knowledge level and job performance (for selected outcomes).

Outcomes vary by targets and set criteria. For example, you may not want "all or nothing" targets for outcomes (if patients are frail elders with diabetes and congestive heart failure, what does "health promotion" mean for them?). What is the specific target for health promotion? Can it be defined in terms of patient function? How broad or how specific will this be? In other cases you will be considering outcomes criteria set by external agencies such as The Joint Commission on Accreditation of Healthcare Organizations (JCAHO), Magnet, or other accrediting agencies. Thinking ahead about important outcomes helps focus project purpose and methods (the additional project triangle points).

GENERAL OUTCOMES-EVALUATION PRINCIPLES

When considering outcomes evaluation, basic concepts can be useful in making project-planning choices. Some points to consider include those in the following paragraphs.

Outcomes Serve a Purpose

Clearly identified outcomes guide you in gaining the correct data rather than a lot of extraneous data. You will have to name outcomes that are effective, efficient, practical, and feasible. Avoid collecting data for the sake of data. You don't want large amounts of evaluation data collected and just stored in an electronic filing cabinet. You want to focus on collecting outcomes data that will be used. Tons of data can be collected and reported, but it is not good if missing the analysis or the "so what" piece. So this involves thinking ahead about who the users are, whether the data addresses issues that are important to the users, and that the data can be presented in a clear understandable format for the users. You want data that are usable versus just collected.

Outcomes Vary by Concepts of Interest

You want to identify outcomes that are as concrete as reasonable for your concept. Some concepts are easier to gain true measures of than are others. For example, physiological measures such as blood glucose are recognized for good reliability and validity. Even so, there are differences in how objectively different outcomes are measured. For example, exercise tolerance measures are more concrete than self-reported symptoms on a patient self-survey. That does not mean there is not value to each measure, but in the proposal you will make choices and need to defend why you are choosing select approaches to evaluate outcomes.

Outcomes Need to Be Identified Prospectively

Why is thinking ahead about outcome issues important? As you cannot ask and answer all evaluative questions, the challenge is to choose useful outcomes data. Ask questions such as, Will gaining selected outcome data be useful? For what purposes? What tools are reasonably available to evaluate selected outcomes?

Selected Outcomes Should Consider Who Needs the Outcome Data

It is important when planning outcomes evaluation to address the who, what, and when. Who needs what information when? And why do they care about these outcome data? For example, as a unit administrator, is there value in creating a staff development program designed to improve patient care outcomes on a documented problem area?

Outcomes Should Have Timelines for When to Evaluate

You should also consider your planned outcomes and determine relevant time factors. In some projects it will be important to consider short- versus long-term outcomes. Many clinical projects first address short-term outcomes and then a follow-up plan to address long-term outcomes. You will also determine if baseline data exists or needs to be gained. In educational terms, you may consider formative versus summative outcomes measures or combinations. The proposal needs to document specifically these decisions.

Technology and Outcomes

Also consider the value of technology when thinking about outcomes. For example, electronic health records have made major strides in accessing outcome data. The minimum data set (MDS) for accessing resident outcomes in long-term care is a good example. Outcomes on the MDS scale, such as weight loss, are captured first on individual patients as part of their electronic record; then these data are compiled with others and can then be compared not only by individual patients but also by facilities with comparisons at state and national levels.

Addressing the "So What" Factor for Outcomes

There are several sources that inform the outcomes that are identified for any given clinical project. These include, among other things, the purpose of your project, the methods of your project (both illustrated by the triangle), and what interests you. They can relate to patient outcomes, staff outcomes, or systems outcomes. As you consider potential outcomes, the "so what" question is important and is further clarified by addressing questions such as:

- What will others do with the outcomes?
- What difference will the project make in improving health, education or health care quality, costs, and, most important, patient, family, or community outcomes?
- Is there probability that this outcome is relevant to others from a feasibility and reproducibility perspective?

Broad Evaluation Principles

As you begin to make plans to evaluate chosen outcomes, a list of principles that can guide outcome evaluation plans/choices is described by the American Association of Higher Education (n.d.). Although these have been framed from a student-evaluation perspective, the principles apply to staff development and in most cases patient evaluation as well. These have been determined to be a form of best evaluation practices. Of note, there is value in multimethods approaches that provide a type of triangulation to evaluation. Using varied methods as well as gaining differing perspectives from those in varied positions can add to the credibility of outcomes data evaluation plans. The principles described by the American Association of Higher Education (n.d.) are paraphrased below.

Outcomes assessment/evaluation works best when

- it begins with broad values statements
- it comes from integrated, multiple perspectives and when it is considered over time
- purposes are clearly stated
- it addresses not only the outcomes but the processes that lead to these
- it is ongoing (as in quality improvement) rather than episodic
- multiple team members are involved
- it involves practical issues that are important to people
- it is used for improvements as part of a larger set of change initiatives
- it meets responsibilities to the public as well as agency stakeholders

MAKING CHOICES ABOUT OUTCOMES

Again related to the project triangle, start by keeping concepts broad and simple; then work toward the level of detail needed for the desired outcome. Name the outcomes you are going for, define them, and then operationalize them (similar to concept analysis as described in Chapter 6).

Sample Outcomes on Varied Concepts

Various measurement choices are available as noted, with broad examples that include costs of care, symptom control, functional status, mortality, and morbidity (Whitman, 2003). These broad outcomes can then be further detailed. Further broad outcome examples follow.

For example, outcomes concepts for broad patient or staff education audiences include the following:

- Behaviors and competencies
- Attitudes and perceptions
- Satisfaction

Examples of useful patient outcomes to consider are:

- Patient satisfaction
- Emotional status
- Physical status/functional status outcomes
- Psychosocial outcomes such as quality of life
- Home/family change/outcomes
- Use of services
- Costs of services

Outcomes evaluation is a large topic with many considerations. This chapter lays out basic considerations. These include outcomes as part of a systems approach and principles that guide good outcomes evaluation.

Also remember to consider outcomes from varied perspectives. Consider from whom you are interested in gaining outcomes. For example, are you interested in the patient's perspective or that of the staff, family, administrators, or interprofessional health team members?

WHAT APPROACHES ARE USED TO GAIN DATA TO LEARN ABOUT OUTCOMES?

There are many approaches from which to choose when gaining data to address your outcomes. Tools including interviews, observations, or document reviews are typical sources of these outcome data. Outcomes data from these varied data-collection methods will need to be reported as such, with strengths and limits of each noted.

Future chapters address strategies such as interview, survey, observation, and document review as components of evaluation plans. Although numerous variations exist in each of these approaches, they provide a good starting point for considering the ideal and real possibilities for evaluating project outcomes.

OTHER OUTCOMES-EVALUATION CONSIDERATIONS

Challenges can exist in naming outcomes and making evaluation plans. Some outcomes will be easier to name than others. Some outcomes will be easier to document than others. Selected points include the following:

- *Challenges with ambiguous terms.* If your project involves concepts such as "increased access" for "high-risk" patients, you will need to be very clear on what these terms mean. What is the general consensus for defining the outcome of increased access? What do each of these terms mean specifically to this project? Other outcomes such as knowledge, satisfaction, and behaviors will present their own challenges in definition. Clarity and consistency in using these in the proposal are needed.

- *Can you show prevention?* Other important outcomes, such as prevention, present their own unique challenges. For example, how will you show you are preventing adverse events and promoting safety and quality? Possibilities exist such as case exemplars of what might happen without an intervention or comparisons to adverse events in previous time periods. What will you do if no good measures exist for measuring your concept? Further discussions with a mentor would be appropriate at this time.

TIPS FOR GETTING STARTED

1. What outcomes would you like to see within your clinical setting or patient population? Taking current data and seeing where unit outcomes stand provide a good starting point for evaluation.
2. What evaluation data are you already gaining in your clinical setting? Which are most helpful in documenting outcomes?
3. Are these outcomes reasonable and realistic? Concrete/measurable? (back to concept analysis,what are you actually talking about)?
4. Will these outcomes be short term? Long term? What challenges still exist? What is still needed?
5. What would you do differently in your current outcomes-evaluation plans or to extend these evaluations?

In later chapters you will read about common project models and common tools used in developing outcomes-evaluation plans for your project proposal. These tools include both qualitative and quantitative approaches to gaining data. Versions of interviews, surveys, observations, and record reviews will be described as common tools for gathering data to document outcomes.

You will address each outcome or each project objective and determine what data will be collected. What tools will be used? What will be the schedule for data collection? Future chapters address more specifics as to "where do data-collection tools come from?" as well as what characteristics indicate their credibility and usefulness?

SUMMARY

Positive outcomes are often related to clinical accountability and serve as indicators of success. Outcomes evaluation is a key component of advanced clinical projects. Projected outcomes are a point on the project triangle aligning with the project purpose and methods.

NEXT CHAPTER UP

The next chapter focuses on naming a specific purpose statement for your plan. The purpose statement serves as a focus and type of contract for your project.

LEARNING ACTIVITIES

Written Reflection

Start with a one-page written reflection that addresses your project purpose. Include potential outcomes choices and identify potential evaluation concerns. Using the project triangle, begin working backward from outcomes you are seeking to identify potential methods for seeking their evaluation.

Recalling Your Experiences

Most have attended and are familiar with continuing education (CE) programs. Think of a recent program and consider what outcomes were evaluated. Were there other outcomes that could have been gained to show value in the program? How would you name and describe those outcomes? What ways might you capture those outcomes? Knowledge test? Planned behaviors survey? Satisfaction with learning? Other?

8

Guiding the Advanced Clinical Project: The Purpose of a Purpose Statement

REFLECTIVE QUESTIONS

The following reflective questions organize learning for this chapter. Which of the following are you most comfortable with?

- What is a purpose statement?
- Why is a purpose statement important?
- How is a purpose statement related to the clinical problem?

WHAT IS THE PURPOSE STATEMENT?

In the previous chapter you identified potential outcomes for your clinical project. Now you'll turn to writing the purpose statement that will address the clinical problem and provide continued direction throughout the duration of the project. For example, if the clinical problem is inconsistency in orienting patients to cardiac rehabilitation, such that vital content is sometimes missed or care is not individualized enough, then the purpose statement should direct the project by addressing that problem and finding an answer. In this case, taking the problem statement to the next level includes generating a purpose statement that guides the project toward resolving the problem with cardiac rehabilitation orientation. You may have to consider solutions or strategies for further study of that problem, and these reflections will lead your thinking and writing to a clear purpose statement for your project. For example, the purpose in this case may be to develop a template to guide development and testing of future new cardiac rehabilitation orientation exemplars.

The purpose statement provides guidance and direction throughout the project. You may propose to develop evidence-based protocols for managing chronic health problems, to develop evidence-based education programs to guide staff in gaining competencies, or to generate new evidence related to unique patient population needs. Regardless of the project proposed, there will undoubtedly be times of confusion and misdirection as you progress. It is at these times that the purpose statement is essential in redirecting focus to the proposed project. For example, lost in the volumes of literature on cardiac rehabilitation, you may find yourself reviewing evidence relating to pediatrics and wondering if that's how you should be spending your time. Return to the purpose statement and determine whether the population identified includes pediatrics or not. If adults are specified in the proposal, then you need to redirect your literature review to focus on adults. If at any time there is a question about the direction in which the project is progressing, return to the purpose statement and see whether there is a match.

THE PROJECT TRIANGLE

The project triangle uses the purpose statement to ensure that the clinical problem is addressed and to keep all elements of the project consistent with one another and with the project as a whole. Recall that the three points represent the purpose statement, methods, and outcomes. As you progress through the advanced clinical project, those three points should remain intact, indicating consistency among the purpose, methods, and outcomes. Note the purpose statement is deliberately positioned at the top of the triangle; it might even be considered analogous to the North Star in providing direction and guidance throughout the project. For example, in the project to develop and test an orientation template for new cardiac rehabilitation patients, one method may include an evidence review of the literature for orientation template development, a cardiovascular exemplar completed with peer review, and then piloting with new patients. When direction is lost or you begin to flounder, which will invariably happen, simply look to the top of the triangle and review the purpose statement. The rest of the project should be consistent with and support that purpose statement.

HOW IS A PURPOSE STATEMENT RELATED TO
THE CLINICAL PROBLEM?

In Chapter 7 you identified an outcome that, if achieved, would address your clinical problem and improve the quality of patient care. The next step is to take that problem statement and outcome and translate them into a purpose statement. In the purpose statement you take an existing clinical problem statement and translate it into a statement that will guide you into a future resolution (outcome) of the problem. Thus, addressing the purpose statement will answer the clinical problem identified (Dusick, 2011) and produce the desired outcome.

Just as naming the problem and reviewing the literature occurred together, as discussed in earlier chapters, the development of the purpose statement also occurs simultaneously with the literature review. As the purpose statement represents the future answer to a current clinical problem, it is important that current information about the problem is known and accounted for in the project. It is also important that enough literature be reviewed to establish the clinical relevance and value of the proposed advanced clinical project. When completed and reviewed, the purpose statement should confirm the focus and value of the clinical project in terms of addressing the identified problem statement and also contributing to the best current evidence in clinical practice.

PROBLEM STATEMENT TO PURPOSE STATEMENT

From Problem to Solution

You are now ready to move from a clinical problem that needs to be addressed in order to improve patient care (your problem statement) to a project purpose that will solve that problem (your purpose statement). For example, the lack of evidence supporting the use of simulation in the hospital orientation of new graduates may be the problem to solve, and generating evidence about the effectiveness of simulation experiences to guide graduate nurses in the 3-month new-hospital-employee orientation would be an appropriate purpose to address that problem.

Although it is preferable for purpose statements to provide details of the project, it may be helpful to first practice the transition from problem statement to general-purpose statement, from problem to solution. Remember the nurse who did not have a consistent or thorough orientation for new cardiac rehabilitation patients? Think about what the solution to that problem would be in order to start writing the purpose statement. In this case, the purpose statement might be: To conduct a comprehensive literature review in order to establish a new orientation protocol. Do you see the transition from a clinical problem (an inconsistent orientation for new cardiac rehabilitation patients) to a project that addresses the problem (a literature review to establish an orientation protocol)? Another example might be stated as follows: You are using simulation to orient new graduate nurses to the hospital, but you are not sure whether it is an effective method of orientation. That problem might translate into the following project-purpose statement: To generate evidence regarding the effectiveness of the simulation experiences for new nursing staff and identify implications for future orientation sessions.

An Optional Approach for Getting Started: The Clinical Question

First steps can be very difficult. When moving from the clinical problem to the purpose statement, you are moving from a problem that needs to be solved to a future project that will address that problem. Sometimes a helpful step in moving from the clinical problem statement to the purpose statement is to first convert the clinical problem into a clinical question, which implies a future response and, in turn, represents your project's purpose. In addition to helping you clarify the desired outcomes of your advanced clinical project, the clinical question can also provide a reasonable starting point for a literature search. Note that the way the clinical problem is stated makes a big difference in the topic that's addressed and the answer that will be found. Melnyk and Fineout-Overholt's (2011) PICOT (population, intervention, comparison, outcomes, and time) questions provide a sample format that demonstrates this principle for reviewing the literature. Perhaps you've implemented simulations into the hospital orientation for new nurses, and the clinical problem you need to address is whether use of simulations provides an adequate orientation experience. Note the nuances in the questions asked below and the answers that will be produced.

- For graduate nurses taking a 3-month new-hospital-employee orientation program, how do clinical experiences versus simulated experiences affect skill acquisition and critical-thinking skills?
- For graduate nurses taking a 3-month new-hospital-employee orientation program, do simulated experiences compared with clinical experiences lead to more accuracy diagnosing at-risk new graduate employees?

- How do graduate nurses in a 3-month new-hospital-employee orientation program perceive simulated experiences?

Again the PICOT questions may guide your literature search and help you identify the level of literature/research evidence available relevant to the clinical problem you've identified. In fact, they may be most useful in guiding the literature review rather than further project direction because of the limited number of well-developed studies in so many diverse areas of nursing. Now reflect on the three clinical questions just posed and consider the purpose statement that might flow from each. For example, if your clinical question is about how graduate nurses perceive simulated experiences, then your purpose statement might read:

- The purpose of this project is to describe how graduate nurses perceive simulated experiences as part of their 3-month new-hospital-employee orientation program.

Keep in mind that different clinical problems and questions can lead to various purpose statements; hence, make sure you write the purpose statement to answer the question you really want to be answered.

Revising Your Purpose Statement

Keep in mind that the first draft of your first purpose statement will not be your final purpose statement. The initial leap from problem statement to general-purpose statement is a vital exercise in transitioning from current problem to future project solution. However, once that initial step is taken, there will likely be multiple iterations as you move from an initial purpose statement to a fully mature and well-expressed purpose statement.

Also be aware that revising your initial statement into a good purpose statement is harder than it might look at first glance. Take, for example, the following statement: The purpose of this project is to develop a teaching tool for new hospital nurses. This statement leaves the reader with more questions than answers. What is the topic of the teaching tool? A teaching tool for a skills lab would be very different from a teaching tool about hospital policies. What level of new nurses? A teaching tool for new graduates would be very different from one for seasoned nurses. Once you have an initial purpose statement written, read it over several times and ask yourself what's missing. That missing information provides direction for your subsequent purpose-statement revisions. After considering the following purpose statements, identify missing information, and revise each statement to provide the missing information.

The purpose of this capstone project is to:

- Implement a new simulation scenario for practicing nurses.
- Improve the quality of care for patients hospitalized in the Midwest.
- Evaluate peer-led support groups for newly diagnosed teenage diabetics.

The Final Purpose Statement

Although it would be nice for purpose statements to answer every who, what, when, where, and how question, that is sometimes not feasible. Minimally, the purpose statement should be honed down to a single concise statement, written explicitly as the purpose statement, which identifies the project topic and population. Preferably it will also include the methods to be used, variables involved, and the setting (Cambridge Rindge & Latin School [CRLS], 2012; Dusick, 2011). A sample purpose statement is as follows: The purpose of this study is to develop an evidence-based protocol regarding the use of simulation experiences to optimize skill acquisition and critical thinking in a 3-month new-graduate nurse hospital-orientation program. Note that this purpose statement includes the topic (simulation), method (evidence based and review of literature), the variables (simulation, skill acquisition, and critical thinking), the population (new-graduate nurses), the setting (hospital orientation), and the outcome (protocol). Again, reflect on the nuances of this purpose statement and the way in which subtle changes might affect the nature of the project and the outcomes obtained.

The final question to ask yourself as you revise and refine your purpose statement is: If I conduct this project, will the clinical problem I started with be addressed or resolved? Assuming skill acquisition and critical thinking are the two outcomes you're interested in, this purpose statement will produce an outcome that answers the clinical problem originally identified, so you are ready to move forward to mapping out your clinical project. But if not, stop now before investing more time in the wrong project and back up to your clinical problem. Rework the previous steps, explore the fine nuances in the clinical question you want to answer, and rewrite the purpose statement until it describes the work you need to do to resolve the clinical problem you initially identified.

CHECKLIST: EVALUATING THE PURPOSE STATEMENT

Recall that the problem statement and outcome are inextricably linked to the purpose statement. After you have written an initial purpose statement, revised it, and decided on your final version, then answer the following yes or no questions:

1. Are you attempting to solve the right problem? Have you looked at the issue from multiple perspectives (such as people, place, and process factors) and considered the best approach for focusing your project?
2. Is the project purpose stated completely? Does it incorporate the proposed population, any proposed intervention, and proposed outcomes?
3. Have you read enough literature relevant to your topic to know that your project purpose has relevance?
4. Is it clear how the project will be limited or focused to make it manageable?
5. Does the purpose statement have the potential for providing important and useful information to improve clinical practice?
6. Does the purpose statement lead to the desired outcome?
7. Is the purpose focused enough to be accomplished with a reasonable expenditure of time, money, and effort?
8. Have you considered potential pitfalls?
9. Will the project have the potential to advance clinical processes or outcomes in an important way?
10. Look at the purpose statement once more and ask yourself: Is this project really what I want to focus on?

If you answer each question with a resounding "yes," then you're ready to move forward. Any "no" responses indicate a need for further reflection and likely additional revisions to the purpose statement.

ADDITIONAL STEPS IN WRITING THE PURPOSE STATEMENT

There are two additional steps in writing a good purpose statement. First, continue to review your purpose statement and make appropriate revisions and repeat this activity on several different occasions. Time does make a difference, so when you believe you have your final purpose statement, come back to it at several different times to make sure it still passes the yes/no questions checklist.

Second, ask a colleague to review your purpose statement and provide feedback. Give this step serious thought, considering the strengths various colleagues have to offer in this process, and decide on those people who have the most to offer. Choose peers who will provide you with honest, if gentle, constructive criticism rather than those who will just provide the easier-to-give (and receive) compliments. With initial lists in hand, begin a thorough process of identifying the best candidates to ask for this important job:

- What are the person's strengths in terms of content?
- What are the person's strengths in terms of interpersonal skills?
- What limitations does the person have in terms of time, content, and interactions?
- Will the person provide honest feedback?
- Are there other factors to consider?

This objective review will likely result in needed revisions that you would otherwise miss. Have more than one other person review the purpose statement, preferably a nurse and a non-nurse colleague, as this offers a broader review and greater variety of perspectives to provide input. Keep in mind that this step may take more time than expected depending on your reviewers' respective schedules, so build that time into your own project timeline.

SUMMARY

This chapter has provided a thorough guide in moving from a problem statement to a purpose statement for your proposal. Consider the significance of the purpose statement and its importance to clinical practice. Would you be enthused about working on this proposal? If it were addressed, would patient care be improved?

NEXT CHAPTER UP

You now have a clearly written purpose statement that links your project to a clinical problem and guides your project as it resolves that problem with the desired outcome. The next step is to map out your clinical project, from the purpose statement to the findings, including all of the intervening activities. Remember that the methods, data, and findings must remain consistent with the problem, outcomes, and purpose statement. Also keep in mind that, while anticipating potential problems and laying the groundwork for your final project paper takes more time now, both will prove to be the most efficient means of implementing and completing your clinical project.

LEARNING ACTIVITIES

To-Do List

1. Think back to Chapter 3 when you identified potential clinical problems and wrote problem statements. Select three of your ideas from that chapter and take the leap from the problem statement (which you previously wrote) to an initial purpose statement. Evaluate your initial purpose statement by asking yourself the following two questions:
   a. Do you see the transition from an existing clinical problem to a project that, if conducted, would address that clinical problem?
   b. If the project were conducted, would it solve your clinical problem?
2. Go back to your three initial purpose statements and ask yourself, What's missing? Is there information about the topic? Population? Methods? Concepts or variables? Setting? Outcome? Make appropriate revisions by adding in the missing information.
3. Review the three revised purpose statements and evaluate each according to the evaluation (yes/no questions) checklist. Make appropriate revisions.
4. Identify three professional peers and ask for their constructive feedback on the purpose statements.

Peer-Review Activity

Place yourself in the role of providing peer review for a colleague's advanced clinical project purpose statement. What suggestions would you make to your colleague for improving these initial purpose statements?

- Implement a new policy for breastfeeding mothers.
- Establish protocols for psychiatric patients.
- Improve safety with elderly patients on the orthopedic unit.
- Reduce medication errors in the extended-care facility.
- Provide better care for patients with anxiety.

9

Mapping It Out, From Problem to Advanced Clinical Project Plan

REFLECTIVE QUESTIONS

The following reflective questions organize learning for this chapter. Which of the following do you have the most comfort with?

- What strategies for framing evidence-based projects are available?
- What is your rationale for proposing varied evidence-based projects?
- How will you begin to outline project-proposal plans?

This chapter is about beginning to design and map out your clinical project proposal. The concept of project design (methods) is key. Designing means setting the stage for the project/study. In many cases, the well-designed clinical project can be one step in a change process for improving clinical outcomes. Multiple models exist to guide evidence-based practice (Melnyk & Fineout-Overholt, 2011). This chapter describes some commonly used examples.

Clinical projects involve using the best evidence and project tools to help improve patient care. They also involve making choices from various possibilities. The primary questions that the clinical project addresses are as follows:

1. What is the problem?
2. What is the current evidence?

3. Given the state of evidence, what will be your project focus or purpose statement?
4. What are the projected outcomes of interest? How will you evaluate what happened?
5. What type of design best helps frame the project? What project approaches will be needed?

As you address your proposal, you have already started to answer questions one through four in previous chapters. For example, as director of continuing education (CE) for the house, you know that more education on palliative care for your long-term-care setting is important. After completing your systematic literature review, you found that although there was broad information/evidence on palliative care, there was limited information on specific topics such as nutrition and eating issues at the end of life. From your work in this area you know this is an aspect of both family and staff concern. So, in summary, you have identified a problem, reviewed the current evidence in the literature, considered possible outcomes, and have written a purpose statement based on the problem and evidence.

Now, in this chapter, you will address questions regarding the state of evidence and, given that evidence, what methods in structuring that project are appropriate. So mapping the plan should fit the problem and status of the evidence. Evidence and theory then serve as starting points to map out your project to meet your selected goals and outcomes. In many ways your project is focused for you by determining the level of quality evidence available. If extensive evidence exists and evidence synthesis is needed, that is one approach. If evidence-based protocols are found that can direct practice, then another approach is indicated. If limited evidence exists, consider theory-based or basic descriptive approaches for helping further to generate evidence.

Mapping out the clinical project proposal also requires you to look at the big picture or sketching out the whole. This helps you look for your best approach to an evidence-based project, as well as potential glitches in the plan that could otherwise be overlooked until too late to make a correction for a meaningful project. It reminds you to assess the level of evidence before determining a project type. It helps you clarify how the project will roll out.

MAPPING IT OUT, WHAT THAT MEANS

From early education experiences, recall that if you don't have a plan or map, it is much harder to find your way. It is important to map out your project proposal so that you don't get lost. In this chapter, you will be working on a big picture or map of your project. Your map helps gain the big picture; further details of more specific methods are described once this map is designed.

Being prospective in mapping the project helps minimize potential problems by gaining early guidance and clarifying proposal expectations; it provides an opportunity to act in advance to deal with anticipated challenges. Although mapping out the project may seem like it takes extra time now, its benefit down the road will prove that the time it takes now to map out the project prospectively usually pays you back with saved time in the long run and definitely reduces the number of problems encountered along the way. Again, to begin mapping, recall the state of the evidence on your topic. You will also consider broad project models such as quality improvement and evaluation to help choose a logical project pathway.

RECALLING THE STATE OF THE EVIDENCE

Before mapping your project plan, you have to consider your problem/ topic and the stage at which the available evidence is currently. That will then direct the project methods and outcomes. What if a concern emerged about pain management for patients with dementia? What approaches to a project proposal would be best? Surveying staff knowledge, synthesizing the evidence, or implementing an evidence-based protocol on pain management might all be possible choices. Which one makes the best sense? For example, if after reviewing the literature on pain-management issues for patients with late-stage dementia, you find the following:

1. Good evidence on the topic in varied articles but they are not well synthesized; then you will focus on developing an evidence synthesis or a summary protocol of available data. This is referred to as an *evidence-synthesizing* project.
2. Extensive evidence and protocols exist on the topic; you will then implement or evaluate an evidence-based protocol in your specified setting, using approaches such as quality improvement. This is referred to as an *evidence-implementing or evaluating* project.
3. Limited articles/evidence on the topic exist; then you will conduct a project that generates evidence, for example, a project that gains information from families/staff about the problem/concept. This is referred to as an *evidence-generating* project.

PROJECT MAPPING: DETERMINING A PROJECT PATHWAY FOR AN EVIDENCE-BASED CLINICAL PROJECT

When writing your project proposal, it helps to identify first a big picture of plans/methods and then focus in on a tight description of a clinical project that can be carried out step by step. The approach for your project proposal (and mapping it out) depend in large part on your literature review and what evidence is available on your topic. The three types of projects noted previously—evidence synthesizing, evidence implementing, and evidence generating—will be used to organize this section as you consider their potential in mapping your project. Appendix 9.A provides a generic template to help you begin your work.

Why Evidence-Synthesis Approaches?

Synthesis of the literature involves making the best evidence easily available to health-professional staff. It can include developing protocols, written guidelines, decision trees, or synthesis articles (see Box 9.1). These systematic reviews of the literature guide clinician decisions, inform patient choices, and help others (professional organizations and payers) better understand and use best clinical evidence. These evidence-synthesizing projects can address populations and systems issues and generate resources to meet their needs. These projects can serve as a step in translating research to practice. New protocols or literature-synthesis publications that promote safe care delivery and products for education and leadership are examples. A summary of an evidence synthesis project relevant to pediatric patients and surgical anesthesia is provided in Appendix C.

Once an evidence-synthesizing approach has been determined, synthesizing the relevant literature is the next step. Outcomes for this type of project include a synthesis document; the synthesis might become a manuscript for educating staff or be developed into a protocol/guide ready for further testing. These products are based on systematic reviews that include a critique of the evidence. The synthesis product is then evaluated before it is recommended as ready for practice. A number of models for developing systematic reviews and further products exist, such as the Stetler model for translating evidence. Melnyk and Fineout-Overholt (2011) describe these models and their similar phases that include:

- Preparation (the systematic literature review that involves search/sort/select/evaluate and then synthesize common findings)
- Validation of the review with some type of expert or process/content review

- Translation of the review for an application of some type
- Evaluation phase for the product

Why Evidence-Implementing and -Evaluating Approaches?

In this case, evidence has already been synthesized into a protocol by a respected source. The question becomes: Does the protocol work in all settings with all specialty populations? Will it work for your setting and population? Evidence implementing and evaluating basically means testing an

---

BOX 9.1

Quick Outline: Proposing an Evidence-Synthesizing Project

Use the following considerations to determine whether the synthesis approach to generating an evidence-based protocol or a manuscript/article is reasonable for your specialty situation.

- *Current available evidence*: If you are finding quite a bit of research literature on your focused problem, are asking questions such as, Is my topic or problem one that has a lot of evidence in the literature? One that is ripe for synthesis of what is known in nursing or other disciplines? One for which I can access sources of best evidence?
- *Possible methods*: Systematic review and synthesis of the literature, including expert review of process and outcomes. You then synthesize recommendations for practice and/or identify needs for further research. The ACE star model provides a visual of moving through these components (ACE, 2013).
- *Further reading*: Chapters 4 and 5 provide an introduction to literature synthesis. Sample further readings include books and resources on synthesizing the literature.
- *Evidence-synthesizing examples*: Examples might include developing a guideline on patient's end-of-life nutrition needs for long-term-care nurses. Or it might include a review of the evidence specific to the needs of pediatric patients with obesity and nursing considerations if they are having anesthesia/surgery (See proposal abstract–Appendix C).

BOX 9.2

Quick Outline: Proposing an Evidence-Implementing and Testing Project

- *Current available evidence*: High-quality evidence exists in the form of a protocol from a well-respected source. You might choose this approach if after reviewing this protocol you wonder if it has relevance and would work on a particular unit or with a particular population.
- *Possible methods*: Quality-improvement strategies, and protocol implementation and evaluation approaches will be typical. You may need experience with quality-improvement–type projects, change projects, or case study approaches.
- *Further reading*: Books and resources on quality improvement, case study, and change theory.
- *Examples*: These might include implementing and testing an established protocol for pain management with patients with dementia. Or you might implement and test a communication protocol in a long-term-care setting (See proposal abstract–Appendix D).

---

established evidence-based protocol. It involves asking questions such as do these protocols work in your specified setting?

These types of projects are often framed as a quality-improvement project, change projects, or a case study/case report approach. The quality-improvement approach, for example, would include showing the need for your identified protocol, the strategy for implementing it, and how it would be evaluated. Appendix D provides an example of testing an established staff/provider communication protocol in a unique long-term-care setting. The case study or case report frame might be another consideration for organizing this type of project. Box 9.2 summarizes this approach.

Why Evidence-Generating Approaches?

You have reviewed the evidence and found limited data on your problem or area of interest. For example, related to an increase in patient falls on the unit, you note that most protocols focus on internal patient factors relevant to falls rather than extrinsic room-safety issues. You believe that an observation survey or interview is needed to gain new evidence and help raise staff awareness of the issue. This involves generating new evidence resources. Nurses are often first to identify new challenges in patient care. Often this is where the need for further data originates. Projects will be identified to ask questions to gain subject perceptions about a problem, knowledge about a problem, or perceived behaviors. Data-collection methods, including observation and document review, can also provide new data to help understand a problem. Box 9.3 summarizes this approach.

BOX 9.3

Quick Outline: Proposing an Evidence-Generating Project

- *Current evidence*: If you find almost no research literature specific to your topic and ask questions such as: Is my topic or problem area one that is new or unique in a selected area with little evidence available to better understand or guide work with the problem? Is there more need for evidence in the practice world?
- *Possible methods*: Strategies to gain basic knowledge/information on a topic from a selected population are diverse. Often you will consider basic descriptive study methods for this project. Sometimes the project may be framed as part of a quality-improvement project. For collecting evidence on a given problem, you might use tools such as needs surveys, environmental scans, guided discussion groups, observation tools, or simple interviews or surveys.
- *Further readings*: Readings from quality improvement and research texts specific to basic descriptive projects are useful.
- *Examples*: If you find nursing assistants in long-term care are frustrated and uncomfortable with palliative care, you might seek evidence to better understand the problem. You might have a guided discussion or collect surveys as to their challenges and strategies in providing end-of-life palliative care. Or, if you have interests in rural health clinics, your approach might include surveying rural nurses about their strategies for managing a rural health population (See proposal abstract–Appendix E).

ADDITIONAL APPROACHES TO GUIDE
THE EVIDENCE-BASED PROJECT

You have considered the type of evidence available for your project. Selecting from further common scholarly approaches will be next. These approaches, sometimes considered big-picture frameworks, can guide your proposal and be integrated along with the evidence-based approaches. It is interesting to note that often there is an overlap in methods used within each of these approaches. Framework examples include quality improvement and change models, needs assessments, surveys, and other approaches.

Quality Improvement and Change Models

Quality improvement involves addressing a pressing clinical issue in terms of solving a problem or improving care. Improvement projects are planned to help promote safe clinical care delivery, interpersonal care aspects, and life quality. Typically the scope is narrow, and the context is a specified unit or setting. Quality-improvement projects make a case for the project need. The project integrates appropriate use of literature/best evidence with real-world practice, that is, articulation of how chart (electronic record review) data from your practice setting match an ideal evidence-based clinical pathway. It can help with articulation of problems leading to less-than-quality care or excess resource use. For example, in a large primary care setting with numerous doctors seeing one another's patients, the problem of consistency in treating patients with the new diagnosis of diabetes could be mapped out using this process.

In another example, you notice the aging of your patient population and the increasing incidence of dementia. Staff seem to lack awareness of how best to communicate with these patients. One strategy will be to assess/confirm this need for staff improvement, identify and implement an evidence-based communication protocol, and evaluate the impact. Population and system issues can be addressed with these quality-improvement–type approaches.

Change projects typically use a traditional change model to guide the project. As part of a plan for a new evidence-based protocol on infection control, a model would guide one in naming the change plan, determining phases for implementation, considering potential barriers as well as facilitators, and determining how to evaluate outcomes. Goals are to minimize the barriers and focus on the facilitators. You will consider these potential challenges and strategies as part of your proposal. Involving staff in this process is a typical consideration in change models. This approach could build on the noted quality model, with additional focus on staff involvement.

Evaluation is also a component of these models. Naming the outcomes to be evaluated (i.e., pain-management improvements) and how these will be measured are key. Additional chapters in this text further address tools that can be used in evaluation. Evaluation projects include generating evaluation questions, determining standards for effectiveness, designing evaluation tools, designating participants, collecting data, analyzing, and reporting (Fink, 2004).

Needs Assessments, Descriptive Surveys, and Interviews

As noted, some projects relate to generating further evidence. Selected approaches to help frame a project include needs assessments and descriptive surveys/interviews. While an overview of these approaches is provided, once project decisions are made, further related references will be needed in guiding the project development.

Needs Assessments

Needs assessments help generate evidence about gaps in what currently exists. These tools provide the opportunity to gain new data to help clarify a problem. These are often the first step in a larger project, that is, the need for a new program in a community or hospital. Sometimes a systems model helps frame a needs assessment, that is, asking questions to determine structures and processes that currently exist and then considering how the new program proposed could build on or add to this.

Descriptive Surveys or Interviews and Related Approaches

These projects can help document knowledge, behaviors, perceptions, or satisfaction. An example would be surveying staff on knowledge about emerging research or seeking their concerns about implementing/changing to a new staffing system. Designing small clinical projects that generate evidence that can provide the basis for learning about an issue can be an important step in further developing larger projects.

Other Approaches

Case Studies

Case studies are another way to frame quality improvement or evaluative clinical projects in one setting. This involves one specific unit (or in some cases one unique patient; sometimes multiple case studies are completed and compared). Case studies can be used to illustrate a problem; consider an approach for solving the problem; or address the need for different clinical approaches, theory applications, or further research. Learning about one family member's perceptions of long years of caregiving for a late-stage Alzheimer's patient is one example (Bonnel, 1996). These projects can suggest strategies for better understanding care needs and generating potential strategies for further testing.

PROJECT MAPPING: THE BIG PICTURE

Back to the Project Triangle

Although proposal components are addressed in separate chapters of this book, there is an interplay among them; components are interrelated, and all are needed for completeness and wholeness of the project. This chapter lays out a sampling of approaches/methods to help organize the project plan. Part of this process is clearly aligning the project purpose with the proposed outcomes and methods.

A broad map saves one from problems down the road if links are made in the project triangle early on. Playing with the project triangle and literature and theory can help you identify where project attention is needed. Project questions to begin proposal deliberations have been noted earlier in this chapter and serve here as a reminder in project mapping: What is the available evidence on your topic? What is the product/process that you will package? What broad approaches may be most helpful in gaining better understanding/direction/guidance? Further examples follow.

For example, as an advanced practice nurse in your hospital's occupational health department, you identify many staff who have problems with excess weight (and you are concerned with how this leads to further health problems and safety issues as well as providing poor role models for patients).

The need has been identified. This is a time for questions:

- Is there an evidence-based protocol available to implement (for helping staff)?
- If not, is there reasonable evidence in the literature that could be synthesized into a protocol?
- Is further evidence needed that could be gained from surveys or interviews with staff?
- What is the best direction for a project proposal?

The same approach could be used if, as an advanced practice nurse (APN), you have identified a need for further resources to offer caregivers of patients with dementia.

- Is there an evidence-based protocol available to implement for helping caregivers?
- If not, is there reasonable evidence in the literature that could be synthesized into a protocol?
- Is further evidence needed that could be gained from surveys or interviews with caregivers?
- What is the best direction for a project proposal?

As you begin to map your proposal plan, further early questions for each of the above examples will include:

- What theories or models have relevance to the situation you are trying to improve? The health belief model or the health promotion model in the first case? A middle range theory on caregiving for the second?
- Will the ideas you are generating lead to a project with important implications or have potential for practice, education, and research that is effective and efficient (time/cost)?

As your project plans mature, further questions you will have to ask are: Is it feasible? Cost effective/efficient in terms of staff time? Acceptable to persons involved such as patients, staff, and providers?

FURTHER CONSIDERATIONS FOR THE PROJECT-PROPOSAL MAP

Adding Further Details

Initially a work in progress, the project map helps fill in the details. It helps answer important project questions such as who, what, when, and where? Now that you have narrowed your problem, placed it in the context of the literature, and considered sample strategies to frame your clinical project, you are ready to brainstorm your more detailed project plan. As you reviewed this chapter, what approaches described could be effective and efficient in addressing your specified problem? What are the broad strategies you might use to map approaches to the problem/topic?

Continue detailing your proposed project plan with additional questions. This work in progress moves forward to a detailed plan and serves as a communication tool with colleagues/mentors and later guides in writing the proposal. As you move to the next decisions with your proposal, sample issues will include the following.

If you go with an evidence *implementation/evaluation* or evidence-generating–type project:

- Who will be the subjects?
- What specific outcomes are being sought?
- What are best methods for collecting data to evaluate?
- What will be the setting?
- Which is most appropriate for project guidelines?

If you go with an evidence-synthesizing project, you are reviewing articles to summarize the best evidence on a topic.

- Although articles are not exactly subjects, you will talk about the numbers and type of articles, and how they were gathered.
- Sample questions to consider would be, What criteria will you use for article selection? What types of articles are acceptable? What review criteria will be used?
- What will be your methods for completing the search?

IS YOUR PROJECT FEASIBLE?

The feasibility of your project will further determine your proposal methods. Feasibility refers to the project being practical or do-able. Create a feasibility checklist for completing the project. Some of the following may belong in the proposal appendix and help make a case for feasibility.

- Detailed work plan and timelines
- Summary of any needed resources and how they will be obtained
- Summary of needed competencies for completing the project and how they are attained
- Access to people, facilities, and situations, including any needed permissions
- Procedure approvals from human subjects committees/institutional review boards (Adapted from Krathwohl & Smith, 2005)

TOOLS TO HELP: FURTHER MAPPING AND OUTLINING

Further mapping involves making the points of the project triangle all mesh/intertwine. Sample tools for brainstorming include visual tools and problem-solving approaches, templates, and writing tools. Decision trails are discussed as an important tool for documenting your project-proposal choices.

Visual Maps and Problem-Solving Models

For those who benefit from a visual perspective, create a visual diagram for what you want to happen. Concept maps are common approaches. For those who think in a more linear fashion, additional approaches to help do this include flow diagrams and linear models.

Use of a problem-solving model such as the basic nursing process can help map plans as well. Questions to consider when mapping:

- Assess: Have you assessed the need for the project?
- Plan: Have you planned tentative methods?
- Implement: Have you considered potential challenges with implementation?
- Evaluation: Have you addressed an evaluation plan?

Reflection, Writing, and Documenting

Reflective Writing

A reflective summary allows you to self-assess and address your concerns or satisfaction with the accomplishments (i.e., noting what still needs to be accomplished as well as highlighting the major accomplishments). Guided reflection can enhance self-evaluation of plans. It can lead to further questions and thoughts for the proposal.

Templates, Filling in the Spaces

Templates provide a type of framework with reminders for each project component. The visual cues help get all pieces and reminders needed to flow together. Consider using a one-page table and filling in the pieces. A project template is provided in Appendix 9.A and an example using the Room Safety Scan Project (Bonnel, 2012) provided.

Decision Trail

A decision trail provides a summary of important activities that have been completed in the process of developing the capstone project (think of this as almost a type of cookbook that allows others to see the process/activities you have used in developing your capstone). This should be specific so that if others choose, they could replicate your procedures in another setting. Another way to think about the decision trail is as a listing by dates of specific activities you have completed for the semester. This is sometimes referred to as an Audit Trail.

Project Mapping: Common Challenges to Avoid

Project mapping and troubleshooting include addressing common practical concerns during the planning phase. Use the following to help think about potential issues with your project during project planning.

- Is it the right-sized project—not too large or small?
- Is this the right time/place/person to address this issue?
- Are there any political issues or legal considerations in the proposed project setting that might impact project implementation?
- The points of the project triangle do not mesh; for example, methods such as data to be collected do not fit the project purpose.
- Plans are too broad or not adequately detailed for others to follow/replicate.
- The setting may be challenging to access.
- The project director has limited background to carry out the project activities.
- Plans to use selected equipment or resources may not be realistic (Leedy & Omrod, 2013).

SUMMARY

You have identified your problem and the literature surrounding this problem. You have started to address the context or setting and population issues. Considering the project triangle, what approach seems the best match? As your project ideas come together, use techniques from this chapter to map out plans that can guide your project.

NEXT CHAPTER UP

As discussed in this chapter, you are working on a big picture or map of your project proposal. The next chapter helps add the further detail of more specific methods to use. In general, this includes data-collection (research) tools and strategies that assist in implementing and evaluating your project. Remember that while components of each of the proposal chapters are addressed separately, there is an interplay among all components; each piece is needed to create a complete, cohesive project.

LEARNING ACTIVITIES

To-Do List

1. Complete the literature review for best evidence on my topic of interest.
2. Determine the type and quality of literature that exists for my problem of interest.
3. Create a possibilities reflection (see following learning activity).
4. Begin mapping my plan through a project template.

Possibilities Reflection

Reflective writing can often help better determine a map of possibilities for detailing a project about a specific problem/topic. Reflecting on possibilities might include the following:

1. To learn more about my problem/topic, I might observe the following activities/situations _____
2. I might talk to the following people _____
3. I might review the following documents/resources _____
4. Various ways to address this problem/topic from a project-methods perspective would include _____
5. The most reasonable way to address this problem/topic from a project-methods perspective would be _____

APPENDIX 9.A: EVIDENCE-BASED-PROJECT TEMPLATE

The following provides a template to begin mapping your project ideas. See the next page for a completed example.

Title of EBP project:				
Problem summary		**Current best evidence**		
Purpose statement		**Proposed project design** **What theory will guide the project?**		
What data will be collected?	What tools will be used to collect this data?	What is the quality of the measure?	Who will collect the data? How will the data-collection methods be systematic and rigorous?	How will the data be analyzed?

EXAMPLE: EVIDENCE GENERATING*

Title of EBP project: *Room Safety Scan*

Problem summary	Current best evidence
Patient falls in clinical setting are a major problem. Literature review suggests intrinsic patient factors are better understood than extrinsic factors.	Although literature summarizing intrinsic patient factors leading to falls is evident, limited data are found about the extent of environmental issues leading to falls.

Purpose statement	Proposed paper/project design
Purpose: To raise awareness of fall-safety issues by systematically observing patient rooms for the presence of environmental safety issues.	Descriptive observational project to promote imroved quality care.
	What theory will guide the project?
	Broad systems theory guides attention to structure and process of care to prevent fall outcomes.

What data will be collected?	What tools will be used to collect this data?	What is the quality of the measure?	Who will collect the data? How will the data-collection methods be systematic and rigorous?	How will the data be analyzed?
Safety factors in 30 occupied patient rooms	Room safety observation checklist	New tool from the literature. Peer review to be completed.	Project director will collect data over 3 weekends.	Descriptive statistics for each safety item and scores as a whole will be reported.

* *Source:* Bonnel, 2012.

10

Writing the Methods Section, Organizing the Advanced Clinical Project Proposal

REFLECTIVE QUESTIONS

In the last chapter you considered the importance of mapping out broad plans for your proposal. The following reflective questions help you consider further development of your methods section and organize learning for this chapter. Which of the following do you have the most comfort with?

- What makes detailing proposal methods important?
- What specific methods are addressed in the proposal?
- What specific approaches could work for your project?

THE IMPORTANCE OF THE METHODS SECTION

This chapter helps identify the big picture regarding research methods for your project. A function of the methods section is to address what you plan to do and why you plan to do that. The methods section describes the process that will be used to get to the project product or outcomes. If you are proposing an evidence-generating or evidence-testing approach for your project, the following elements need to be described:

- Setting: Specify elements of the specific setting in your project.
- Population: Specify the population you will study, giving at least a broad description of participants.

- If intervention is to be used: Describe the intervention and its component parts in sufficient detail that others could reproduce it; outline initial plans for how the intervention is to be implemented.
- Data collection: Describe the specific data-collection plan.

Let's say you are working with patients with Parkinson's disease (PD) and want to develop a project related to support groups for those patients. As you read through this chapter, refer to Box 10.1 and think about the initial challenges presented in project planning. Note any similarities/differences to this project and the one you are working on.

Writing a project proposal incorporates many components. Key in aligning these components is the project triangle. This chapter focuses on the methods point of the triangle and helps address "how do I do the methods?"

BOX 10.1

Methods Example: Parkinson's Disease Online Support Group

If you were working with patients with PD and were concerned about their emotional support issues, what are some of the problems/issues that come to mind? What are some potential responses by health care providers?

Your response of course is to head to the literature to gain answers. You will have to first review the literature to determine best evidence for support groups as a resource. What questions come to mind?

- Based on the evidence available, should you recommend support groups or are further questions raised? What do you still need to know?
- Does your evidence address the changing needs of patients who are progressing through the disease? Does the literature cover all disease stages, or are there special needs for patients with later stages of the disease?
- Does your literature address the setting/access/context for support groups. Does the literature address advancing PD and online versus face-to-face group strategies/challenges?
- Based on the literature, what are your options for framing a project?

FOCUSING THE PROJECT METHODS

Project methods will vary depending on the project approach you choose. For example if you are evaluating a new protocol, that will involve implementing an intervention. When intervention is to be used in your project, outline initial plans for how the intervention is to be implemented. Describe the intervention and its component parts in sufficient detail so that others could reproduce it. Squire's (n.d.) guidelines address components to include such as who will implement the intervention (individual or multiple), and what are their qualifications (or the methods needed to train them)? Are there any issues concerning internal validity of the project intervention and are plans for monitoring the fidelity of the intervention in place? Evaluating the protocol will also include data collection.

PLANS FOR GAINING DATA

Plans for gaining data provide one of the most interesting parts of the project proposal. It is here that you devise plans to organize information/ evidence in new ways to learn new things about a topic. This is central to clinical scholarship. To make sure you have good data to share, you need good methods for data collecting/organizing. Approaches to be considered in this chapter include (1) interview/survey, (2) observations, and (3) document or electronic record reviews. A review of these topics from your previous coursework is provided in quick summary format, including common challenges and benefits.

As you generate the methods section of your proposal, you will have to describe tools that help you gain data/evidence to best solve your problem. Using problem-solving models is one approach. For example, nursing process is a problem-solving model that reminds one to assess for need, name the problem, plan the project response, implement, and then evaluate. Consider what approaches to data collection (interview, observation, and record review) can best help gain data to address your project. Both qualitative and quantitative approaches to using these tools are also considered.

METHODS FOR GAINING DATA: THE PROJECT TRIANGLE

Making the methods choices fit with the project purpose and desired project outcomes is the goal. Recall the triangle, in which the purpose, methods, and outcomes represent the three points. Any inconsistency among the three will make the triangle fall apart, as the three lines won't match up into the shape of a triangle. Therefore, a key aspect is keeping those three components—purpose, methods, and outcomes—in alignment with one another.

The purpose statement will be based on the problem and current evidence found in the literature, and provides the basis for an evidence-generating, synthesizing, or implementing/testing-type project. Again there needs to be consistency between the purpose, methods, and outcomes you choose for your project.

In going back to the project triangle, your project purpose dictates the types of methods needed for a complete/quality project. Ask: What has the purpose statement promised? This guides choices for data collection and sampling. For example, when you plan to collect project data, you will be making choices about interviews, surveys, observations, document reviews, or some combination thereof.

Gaining Project Data Through Selected Tools

Gaining project data involves determining the "what and when" or what information is needed about the specified population. How can that data best be gained? Consider broad choices and then further detail can be added later. Making choices about common tools for gaining project data include considering interview, survey, observation, and/or document-review opportunities and determining the best qualitative or quantitative approaches to use. You have to use the best methods possible to get the best results. Weak pieces in the methods section lead to weak project outcomes.

Preparing a detailed plan and negotiating the best tools/approaches to take while keeping in mind the practical resources available are all considerations in planning your methods. Again you will consider the evidence available concerning this problem to determine what type of project will best assist in improving patient care. You reviewed the literature and gained ideas from what others have done; now it is time to explore project methods and consider options for an effective, efficient project. Your purpose statement will guide your project methods/tools.

WHICH METHODS FOR DATA COLLECTION WOULD WORK BEST?

The project purpose you choose influences the methods you use. For example, if your purpose is to generate evidence on a new clinical challenge, then you might choose either a qualitative or quantitative survey approach to gain data about that challenge. As you recall, within the qualitative or quantitative paradigms, various common data-collection methods include interviews, surveys, observation, or document reviews. The following paragraphs first consider qualitative versus quantitative approaches to methods. Then common tools used within both qualitative and quantitative paradigms, interviews, surveys, observations, and document reviews are discussed.

Qualitative Context: Issues to Consider

The qualitative paradigm considers the world through a lens of openness and complexity. The value of broad open-ended questions directed by qualitative paradigms includes gaining perspectives from the subject about his or her perceived knowledge, attitudes, and behaviors. Qualitative methods typically include gaining some type of word data, as opposed to numeric data. Themes summarizing the data are typically reported.

Qualitative methods provide a beginning toolkit for gaining data that can be authentic and meaningful. Well-known qualitative tools such as interview and observation bring real-world experiences to life through the written word and provide descriptive richness for data sharing. Qualitative data can help describe and make a compelling case for work in early descriptive stages. It can serve as the basic descriptive data for sharing and developing future projects. Qualitative methods capture word themes that convey experiences in a richer texture than quantitative numbers alone.

Benefits of qualitative methods include gaining subjects' true understandings from their perspectives. A depth of understanding missing from numerical summaries can be gained. Typically a small sample size will be beneficial in learning about others' experiences, for example, interviews of those new to a role like geriatric nurse practitioner (Bonnel, Belt, Hill, Wiggins, & Ohm, 2000). Qualitative approaches also provide opportunities/benefits to make broad observations such as windshield surveys and walk-through areas in new or unique settings. Theory is often used to help organize these initial observations.

Challenges to qualitative approaches include the small sample sizes used, which often limits the ability to generalize the findings. These are typically descriptive projects that do not focus on testing hypotheses.

Sample uses/approaches include broad open-ended interviews either with individuals or with groups. It can also include surveys with broad open-ended questions or use of broad observation guides for a specific setting or behavior. The same goes for document reviews. Often approaches are used to study new topics or areas with limited research. They are often used for projects that are evidence generating. They are also used to gain qualitative perspectives in evaluative projects.

Quantitative Context: Issues to Consider

The quantitative paradigm is considered to be focused and deterministic; often this approach is compared to a closed system. Quantitative approaches are used to capture and summarize knowledge, attitude, or behaviors. This involves using tools to gain numerical data representing these qualities, as opposed to word data. These tools provide an opportunity to gain data that can help one understand the numerical qualities of an attribute. Surveys and other tools for observation and document review help specify through numbers what is going on or enable the researcher to make comparisons. A challenge to this method is finding measures or survey instruments that truly capture the concepts being studied. Quantitative approaches lose the richness of descriptive themes gained with qualitative methods but have the benefit of more easily conveying or comparing numerical data about diverse groups.

Quantitative approaches can also help describe and make a compelling case for work in early descriptive stages. Quantitative methods capture numeric summaries that promote ease of comparison. Quantitative approaches help summarize large groups of responses, more easily than qualitative themes. A quantitative approach is often useful in data collection for projects that involve implementing and evaluating a new protocol.

STRATEGIES FOR COLLECTING/GAINING DATA

Qualitative and quantitative paradigms provide the broad context or background assumptions for the choices you make in gaining data. These paradigms set the stage for the more detailed data-collection plan (to learn about the problem or topic of interest). How many ways are there to collect data? To keep things simple, broad approaches of interview/survey, observation, and record review (i.e., charts or electronic health records [EHRs]) are discussed. Further choices and detail then need to be added to each. Further information about these common tools for gaining project data follows.

Interviews and Surveys

Interviews and surveys provide an opportunity to gain information about peoples' knowledge, attitudes, or perceived behaviors. Interview guides and surveys can be developed from either qualitative or quantitative perspectives. Qualitative methods more typically use open-ended questions with verbal responses. Quantitative approaches are more typically closed-ended questions seeking some type of response with numerical coding potential.

- *Face-to-face, individual interviews*: These provide an opportunity to converse with an individual about a specific topic, typically to gain others' perceptions. They include the value of engaging in nonverbal communication about the topic/questions. Opportunities to extend questions and generate follow-up responses to questions that emerge can be valuable.
- *Face-to-face, group interviews*: These provide benefits of gaining individuals' thoughts on a topic. They also provide further opportunity to stimulate ideas from others with brainstorming-type approaches to gain ideas/topics individuals may not have thought to share. Challenges may be to make sure the investigator receives a true opinion versus "group think."

Written Surveys

Written surveys provide the opportunity to learn from others' knowledge or experience related to a topic. They can be easy to administer, but a disadvantage they share is they offer no opportunity to follow up or clarify why the individual responded as he or she did. Also much piloting work is required to make sure participants interpret and respond as the investigator intends.

Planning for Interviews or Surveys

When considering interviews or surveys, basic decisions include: Are well-developed tools available? Are these appropriate qualitative or quantitative approaches? Do they adequately address the concepts of interest? Tool descriptions are further addressed in other chapters.

You also need to plan and be very specific in your proposal about the specific strategies you will use in completing the interviews or surveys. For example, what will be the context or setting for the written, or face-to-face, data collection. Where will this happen? Will there be privacy if this is a sensitive subject? Will there be time during a scheduled clinic waiting time or before a class? How will participants return these forms to you? Online surveys are another consideration. They add to the speed of data collection as long as participants can easily access and have motivation to complete the survey.

Observations

Observations allow opportunities to view activities in natural settings (Warren & Karner, 2005). An observation provides an opportunity to learn new information or confirm concepts and processes. Observations have value in learning about situations, competencies, and behaviors. Observing classrooms or clinical agencies, the investigator learns about roles, practices, and strategies of people they observe and also gain information about the setting's structure and processes. Observations may be used less frequently than surveys and interviews, but they are valuable in learning real-time behaviors. Specifying or mapping out and documenting a plan that includes time or event factors to observe allows better opportunity to capture what is intended. For example, in an early project, Bonnel (1993), using a qualitative format, completed an observation of a group dining experience for long-term-care residents; a very detailed plan for observations included length of time, the observer's role, and specific schedule of observations. Observation data can also be collected in more structured settings like skills labs. Hober (2012), for example, observed students' experiences in a simulation lab to seek concepts of clinical judgment as part of the simulation. Clinical lab observations also provide opportunities related to staff development and competency assessment.

Record or Document Reviews

A common data-collection strategy, especially in quality improvement, has always been chart reviews. This is a nonintrusive strategy for collecting data. Although typically this was done on hard copies of charts, electronic health records (EHRs) have now emerged.

EHRs have changed the ways of doing chart reviews and provide many advantages. Speed of review is one. These tools fairly rapidly provide collections of data that in the past would have taken hours. It is important to remember that just as chart-review projects included a data-collection sheet, the electronic equivalent is still required. Random questions of the data will not meet the project needs. You will need to give thought to how you structure your electronic "data-collection" guide.

Chart reviews can provide challenges to data collection. Challenges or disadvantages to EHRs and other forms of written record review include that the clinician/researcher has no control over the data that were collected. For example, if you are reviewing care processes, there may be inaccuracies in the recording; that is, something might have actually been done but not charted. Or, if physiologic measures such as blood pressures are gained (usually fairly strong credible measures), there is no control over the protocol used in gaining these measures. Also there is no ability to ask further questions about missing data.

Advantages or benefits of electronic records data include reasonable access to clinical data that can help answer, in particular, quality-improvement questions. Other databases, such as the National Database of Nursing Quality Indicators, also exist, which can be valuable in collecting meaningful data for specified project purposes.

ADDITIONAL COMMENTS ON DATA COLLECTION

Again, for each data-collection method (interviews, surveys, observations, and record reviews), there are many variations related to the structure of items (i.e., highly structured questions through quantitative paradigm versus the open-ended structure of the qualitative paradigm).

The methods discussed can also be combined in useful/appropriate ways. A good research text can provide further detail to guide your additional decisions. With all cases of collecting data, addressing appropriate human subjects and Health Insurance Portability and Accountability Act (HIPAA) guidelines is required as discussed in future chapters.

Box 10.2 provides further examples. Each of these tools can be considered from both qualitative and quantitative perspectives. As you review, consider how many ways there are to use each of these; this is the fun part!

BOX 10.2

Data Collection Tools

Samples used in interviews, surveys, observations, and document reviews include:

	Sample Approaches	Your Examples?
Surveys	Face to face written E-mail or traditional mail Electronic survey	
Interviews	Personal face to face Group guided discussions	
Observation	Clinical labs Clinical setting Public settings	

Consider also how each might (or might not) be relevant to the project you are planning. Examples using the project triangle follow.

PROJECT TRIANGLE EXAMPLES

Evidence Generating

- *Purpose*: To determine need for an onsite health clinic at a large assisted-living clinic.
- *Methods*: Qualitative observations of setting (people and place factors); qualitative interviews with staff/residents about current processes and additional need.
- *Seeking outcomes*: Needs assessment summary documents required for planning an onsite clinic.

Evidence Implementing and Testing

- *Purpose*: To determine success of a new evidence-based discharge protocol for patients with congestive heart failure (CHF).
- *Methods*: Qualitative/quantitative survey of patients and a family member on readiness for discharge; guided discussion with staff on challenges/strategies for using the protocol.
- *Seeking outcomes*: Documented successful protocol or needed improvements.

SAMPLE AND SETTING CONSIDERATIONS FOR YOUR PROPOSAL

Identifying clearly in your proposal the setting and the population your project will study are key to helping your reader gain context. Consider the following setting and population issues as you make these plans and write up these sections.

Clearly Describe the Setting

To describe the setting, you will specify elements of the specific setting in your project. For example, if you want to consider the benefits of "educational gaming" as a strategy for an education-related problem in a large health care system, the education protocol could be placed in the context of all staff education, health-professions education, nursing-student education, or nursing-staff-development education. It could also be placed in the frame of one clinical unit, a large health care system, or systems across a state or the country. Clearly framing your setting (and sample) helps focus your project.

To describe the context or setting for your project, you can first create a big-picture description or "systems" perspective of the overall setting and then fill in the parts/details such as the relevant people factors, place factors, and process factors related to the issue/topic. For example, in a study of a particular long-term-care unit, you might identify the types of rooms, the number of people in the setting, common unit activities, and other factors relevant to your project. You might address what makes this unit similar or different from others.

Clearly Describe Sampling Choices

Will there be subjects? Who will be the subjects? How will subjects be selected to participate in your project. Making informed choices about potential subjects for data collection is an important proposal component. What populations or clinical entities will provide you the information you need? An entire population or selected subgroups? Once you have answered these questions, to describe your potential population you will provide at least a broad description of the population of interest.

For example, related to the initial case interests with Parkinson disease (PD) support groups for patients, to identify your population varied considerations are needed. Some of the descriptive components of and questions related to the population of study should include:

- Who is the broad population of patients with PD in your region of interest?
- Who is the accessible population? Are there currently groups that involve patients in the beginning, middle, or late stages of the disease?
- Will these individuals be in groups that are online or face to face? Do the groups involve caregivers, families, or patients only (or a mix)? Are there other unique population factors that should be considered, for example, young versus older patients?

Sampling Issues

Consider the different options in sampling choices and make the choices complementary to the methods chosen. For example, random sampling provides value in meeting assumptions for more sophisticated statistical procedures. In general, samples with larger numbers are more representative of the population of interest. Assumptions for quantitative statistics, for example, indicate at least an N of 30 to represent the population.

In qualitative projects, typically the convenience sample rules. In early descriptive stages of study, a small N is considered acceptable. Smaller numbers can still provide important descriptive information to help understand a topic or learn about populations' needs. For example, if you are asking rural nurses about challenges and approaches they use to best support patients in settings with scant resources, a sample size of 10 could provide good beginning descriptive data. A qualitative project can help describe and make a compelling initial case relevant to the problem. Further discussions about numbers and statistics required for project analysis are discussed in future chapters.

How will your sampling choices relate to your projected outcomes and analysis? These choices play a major role in determining to whom the results of your project may be relevant. This applies, for example, if you want to make the case that your results have implications beyond your population and setting (e.g., extending findings to another unit or hospital in another region).

Making a good sampling choice will involve knowing your project plan, and the strengths/weaknesses of each approach. Additionally it is critical to consider whether the preferred approach is actually do-able. Sometimes there are trade-offs between the preferred and the do-able; you as the project investigator, make the case for why you make the choices you make.

Quick Questions to Consider to Determine Whether You Will Have Sampling in Your Project

Ask yourself whether you have addressed each of the following:

- Is the population clearly defined?
- Is the population accessible?
- Are choices of convenience or random sampling justified?
- Are sampling procedures sufficiently detailed for replication?
- Are sampling choices appropriate to the purpose statement/project question?

SO WHICH APPROACHES FOR YOUR PROPOSAL?

This chapter talks broadly about methods. But which methods you choose will relate most closely to the type of clinical project design you focus on. As you consider your topic, think back to any similarities with the

PD support group example. As described in Chapter 9, selected ways to use the best evidence for projects include:

Evidence synthesis: Does literature/evidence exist about support groups that has not been synthesized for patients with PD? Would evidence lead to protocols for online groups or face-to-face groups? These could be possibilities. . .

Evidence testing: Does evidence exist in the form of a protocol for chronic care support groups that could be evaluated specifically for PD? Could the protocol be further validated as successful by participants or providers? These could be possibilities. . .

Evidence generating: Is more evidence needed related to specific concerns about groups for patients with PD? Could you ask clients in support groups their opinions? Could you ask clinical providers their opinions? Would possibilities exist for using interviews or surveys to gain further data? These could be possibilities. . .

Again, once the literature has been evaluated and a purpose statement determined, your project purpose will guide the methods you use. Within those larger paradigms of qualitative approaches and quantitative approaches, choices about surveys, interviews, observation, or document review will also be considered. Begin to map out the triangle with appropriate methods to develop proposal plans. Guidance for the appropriate use of methods for the type of project you're conducting is developed with a mentor.

WRITING UP THE METHODS

Where and how does the methods section fit in the proposal? The common scholarly "parts" can help organize your project methods. Describe specifically in your plan the following as part of your methods section:

- Setting—Specify elements of the specific setting in your project.
- Population/Sampling—How is the population defined (inclusion/ exclusion criteria)?
- Sampling—Specify the population you will study giving at least a broad description.
- Specific project implementation plans and evaluation methods— Describe the intervention and its component parts in sufficient detail that others could reproduce it.

Creating a table of contents can serve as a helpful guide in organizing key components of the methods section. If you are in school as you complete your project, the school often has set guidelines for the specific headings to be completed for the proposal. If you are in a clinical agency with specific criteria to be addressed before submission to the Human Subjects Committee, that needs to be addressed as well. If yours is a clinical proposal to seek funding, funding agencies typically have outlined specified categories. Turning the guides into headings when possible helps the reader and typically improves the quality of the product. As previously noted, an abstract or two-page plan draft can keep the proposal tightly packaged for discussions and decision making by team members.

PROJECT METHODS, QUICK QUESTIONS

If you are collecting data for your clinical project, does your proposal address each of the following?

- Does it have methods that fit the project purpose and proposed outcomes?
- Does it provide a description of the population and a strategy for sampling?
- Does it specify procedures for data collection?
- What is its timeline?
- Have you verified resource accessibility?
- Have you resolved any Human Subjects and Institutional Review Board issues?

SUMMARY

This chapter talks broadly about methods and choices for use in clinical project proposals. Qualitative and quantitative paradigms provide background for common data-collection choices of interviews, surveys, observations, and record reviews. The methods you choose will relate to the purpose and outcomes you plan to focus on. As noted, there are multiple approaches to these topics. Various choices keep clinical projects interesting and echo the importance of identifying early on exactly what you need and want to do.

NEXT CHAPTER UP

As you consider approaches to data collection, you are also thinking ahead to how you will gain credible data. You will consider strategies for data collection that promote confidence in the tools chosen for your project and help to ensure that the resultant findings are reliable and valid.

LEARNING ACTIVITIES

Pulling Together Methods and Sampling, Case Example

Based on the readings, what strategies could you suggest to enhance sampling and project methods/approaches (dependable data, reasonable size project) for the following case?

In your hospital, you want to implement and evaluate an evidence-based strategy for communication tips to prevent agitated behaviors in residents with dementia. Which strategies are best to begin?

- A large hospital-wide program? Piloting/evaluating on one medical unit? Other choices?
- Who would you collect outcome data from? What type of data? What would be your methods for data collection?
- How could you set this plan up with the points of the project triangle (purpose, methods, and outcomes)?

Reflecting Further on Your Project Plans

- At this point what seems to be reasonable and work well for the plan you are considering?
- What other options might work as well?
- Address the pros and cons of each of your ideas. What will best meet your planned purpose? What will work best given your context and experience?

To-Do List

1. Complete further reading related to specific approaches you would like to use in your project. Look at examples of other projects that have been completed using similar methods.
2. Consider how you will best access the people or physical resources needed to complete your project.
3. Consider the "so what" or why-this-is-important factor related to your proposed plans.

11

Being Systematic and Objective in Gaining Credible Clinical Project Data

REFLECTIVE QUESTIONS

Data collection is often a central component of clinical projects. In previous chapters, you considered the importance of developing broad data-collection plans for your project proposal. The following reflective questions help you consider further development of your methods section and organize learning for this chapter. As you make a plan for gaining the data, which of the following do you have the most comfort with?

- Why is it important to address detailed plans for data collection?
- What procedures can help you make a plan that is systematic and objective?
- What strategies will you use to promote confidence in tools used and the resultant findings?

When writing a project proposal, addressing the quality of the data to be collected is central. This includes discussing the credibility of tools for data collection and protocols for data collection. Being systematic, objective, valid, and reliable are key considerations.

Also key is aligning these components in the project triangle. Building on the varied project plans previously described, this chapter focuses on further detailing the methods component of the project triangle. This builds on earlier discussions of qualitative and quantitative approaches to interviews, observations, and record reviews. Specific plans for collecting data in systematic, valid, and reliable ways are described in this chapter. This involves clearly describing the properties of the data-collection tools and identifying systematic, replicable protocols for data collection.

WHY A DETAILED PLAN FOR DATA COLLECTION?

Why address the specific how/when/what of data collection? The plan for collecting data should make clear statements about what data are to be collected and how the data will be collected. It is helpful to first recall where the proposal-writing process has already taken you and the decisions made. This includes seeking data as part of the big picture of purpose/methods/outcomes. This chapter further addresses gaining data that are accurate and meaningful. With the big picture in mind, it is time to move on to the specifics of data collection with a focus on your clinical project and components that need to be addressed as part of your plan.

With Your Clinical Project in Mind

What qualitative or quantitative approaches or tools will you be using? How will you describe your tools and your protocols?

- For example, will you be using survey or interview questions that measure factual knowledge, attitudes, and behaviors or questions that identify subjective states or perspectives?
- Or will you be using observations or document reviews to gain data about a specified concept/issue?

Once you decide how data will be collected in your project, you will be describing in your proposal both the tools to be used and the specific protocol or approaches to be followed that can ensure data adequacy and quality. This includes naming specifically what data are to be gathered and the tools to be used in doing this, as well as describing the protocol that will be followed in gaining the data. The following paragraphs further detail how your proposal needs to describe the instruments for data collection and the protocol you will follow. The more complete and thorough job you do now, in respect to proposed data-collection steps and anticipated problems, the easier the actual implementation of data collection will be later on. This part of your proposal must contain very specific information about data collection, including trustworthy tools, and procedures for implementing.

DESCRIBING CREDIBLE/TRUSTWORTHY TOOLS

For others to value your work, they need to understand how you have gained the data. You must describe the instruments used and the reliability and validity of these tools (see Box 11.1). In describing the data-collection tools/ instruments, at minimum it is necessary to:

- Share a thorough description of the tools
- Share any reliability and validity for the tools that have been reported in the literature

Share a Thorough Description

Name the tool you plan to use and describe briefly the historical development of the tool, including when and how it was developed. Describe examples of other projects that have used this tool. Include strengths and weaknesses of the tool. For example, if you are addressing "caring" approaches of critical care nurses, your survey could be a tool developed from Watson's work that addressed the 10 carative factors (Nelson & Watson, 2011). Each item has a 4-point range 1 (low) to 4 (high). You would report this description and then provide examples of how other studies have used this tool. This would include further discussion of the tool's qualities, including reliability and validity.

Share Reliability and Validity

"Reliability" and "validity" are common research terms. The approaches to reliability and validity vary, depending on the type of project to be done. The concept of reliability means methods are dependable or replicable, and the concept of validity means the methods are truthful representations of the data. In describing survey reliability, a common measure to note is internal consistency reliability or Cronbach's alpha. This indicates how well or reliably the tool has "worked" in previous studies. Any concepts of validity described in the literature are also noted (such as construct- or criterion-related validity from previous work on the tool).

Sometimes when projects use qualitative tools, reliability and validity are described using alternate terms. While terms are not standardized, in general the term trustworthiness considers the concepts of credibility, dependability, and confirmability of qualitative data. Potential for transferablity of the project findings is also considered (Polit & Beck, 2012).

BOX 11.1

Describing the Instruments

Example 1: Electronic Health Record (EHR) Survey

For a simple survey, description might begin as follows: This project will use a survey consisting of both close-ended responses and broad open-ended questions that were developed from items identified in the review of the literature. The questions for this descriptive survey included 12 questions. First, background questions about students' opinions are asked and then open-ended questions seeking further clarification of students' ideas are posed. There are 10 structured-response questions about EHRs (4-point rating) and 2 open-ended questions. Potential total scores for the 10 structured items range from 10 to 40 (high rating). The full questionnaire is provided in Appendix 11.A.

Example 2: Health Behaviors Survey

For a more developed survey, description might begin as follows: A tool developed by Walker, Sechrist, and Pender (1987), HealthPromoting Lifestyle Profile II, will be used to measure health behaviors. This is a 52-item scale that addresses 5 subscales of health, including physical activity, nutrition, health responsibility, stress management, and interpersonal relationships. The 52 items are answered with a 4-point response to indicate subjects' personal habits (never, sometimes, often, and routinely). The authors reported high internal consistency reliability, and construct validity was confirmed by factor analysis. Further studies have used this tool and also reported greater than .90 reliability.

Other Tools-Related Issues

Further methods of assessing confirmability include the audit trail you have already started to name project decisions. As you recall, audit trails are objective progress records that document processes and decisions from project beginning to end. This is sometimes called an audit trail because someone could audit your project decisions or pathway.

The concept of *triangulation* also has relevance to a credible project. Related to a specific phenomenon, triangulation involves gaining two or more kinds of data, for example, gaining both interview and observation data. Using more than one method to obtain a similar result improves the strength of the data (Leedy & Omrod, 2013).

Describing the Procedure/Protocol for Implementing

After naming and describing the data-collection tools, you need to indicate a protocol for how the tools will be used in your project. The protocol addresses the specific methods for gaining baseline data and any repeated measures. This section of your proposal involves trustworthy implementation of the protocol for data collection. It is almost a "cookbook"-type approach that someone could replicate. The protocol addresses the what, how, and when questions. For a survey of students, the brief protocol could include the following: senior-level students will be given the survey and an informed-consent form at the end of a specified class early in the spring semester. The purpose of the survey will be broadly described to the students, and they will be asked to complete the survey and then return it at that time. Students will not receive points for completing the survey and there will be no consequences for choosing not to participate in the survey.

Or, in another example, if your project involves a patient room safety observations checklist, you would have already noted a tool with good reliability and validity or gained content expert review of a checklist developed from review of the literature. Additional plans to be described in the proposal include approaches such as specified observation data from the "safety checklist" gained from 10 occupied rooms each weekend over a period of 3 weeks. The safety checklist will be completed by the project director. As can be noted, the protocol further defines the observations. Others for example might want a project that observes over weekdays to see whether similarities or differences exist.

Similar protocols are needed to plan for interviews or when handing out written surveys. Protocols provide enough direction that others could critique a protocol's strengths/weaknesses, or they could replicate the protocol in a similar setting.

Pilot Testing of Tools/Methods

As you make plans for consistent, reliable data collection, pretesting or piloting your tools and procedures can help identify any potential problems (Box 11.2). Before you hand your survey to 50 people, you want to make sure the setting, procedures, and the survey itself will make them comfortable in responding.

It is important to pilot or pretest your survey form. Good survey items provide a full range of answers to the participants, who are then willing to provide honest answers. For example, if you are using a qualitative survey and ask, "Could you share an experience about a safety issue?" some respondents might respond yes and then move on. This phrasing, if not caught in a pilot test, would make you miss the rich data you were seeking. Piloting would remind you to rephrase this, changing the instruction to, something like "please share a sample experience." Another consideration to keep in mind: If you ask about certain benefits and all respondents answer "none," you are also missing data. It is often useful to add a survey question like "What else would you like to say about this topic?" or "What other thoughts do you have on this topic?"

How many people should you include in the pilot? Although no numbers are given, at least three people would give you a small range of experiences to get diverse feedback/perspectives. In addition to piloting surveys, you should also pilot observation checklists or document review forms so that others who might use these can help clarify any fuzzy points prior to their data collection (Leedy & Omord, 2013).

BOX 11.2

Quick Tips for Data Collection

You should use good tools and be systematic in using them. Points to consider:

- Describe instruments and procedures (qualitative, quantitative, or mixed) that will be used to gain data or assess the effectiveness of an implementation.
- Report efforts to validate and test reliability of assessment instruments.
- Describe the protocol for collecting the data.
- Additionally, include any needed methods for training others in data collection and piloting the data-collection plan.

OTHER CONSIDERATIONS

Potential challenges exist in data collection. Address each of the following as part of your methods section to promote an efficient and effective project (Krathwohl & Smith, 2005).

The Setting

Name your setting for data collection. If you plan to have students complete surveys electronically during class, you have to ensure that on a particular day, time, and place, students would bring or have access to their electronic devices for data entry. Further evaluating sites for access and appropriateness of the project and data collection are described in other chapters.

Data Organization

As data are collected, you will need plans that include logging the data. For example, if 50 surveys and 20 questions are answered by hand, the stack of 50 surveys will not be useful to you. Your proposal should indicate who will transcribe data and what type of timeline will be used. In many cases, this will include first transcribing to a program such as Excel, so that you can review data for completeness and any patterns in responses. Then in most cases, you will have to transfer the data to a software program such as SPSS for computing further analyses.

Storing Data

Also address where you will store the collected data. It is especially important to note plans to store your data in a secure place, typically a locked file that others cannot access; this is required if you ensure confidentiality of the data. Further issues in ensuring data confidentiality are addressed in other chapters.

Data-Collection Timeline

Your proposal needs a timeline to guide and promote consistency in data collection and progress (Krathwohl & Smith, 2005). This timeline includes attention to the who, what, and when of data collection. For example, if you are seeking to survey graduating student nurses on their readiness to practice in a culture of safety, your survey would need to be administered while they were still finishing courses. An error in timelines (or not planning far enough ahead for human subjects) could miss the data-collection point or postpone it by a full semester or even a year. Have a specific timeline in mind that determines when is the best time to collect your data and is even as basic as whether you can bring snacks to that classroom.

Technology and Data Collection

There are both benefits and challenges in using technology in data collection. Benefits include rapid access to surveys for participants and easy access to collected data for the project director. Challenges include ensuring that all participants have easy access to the technologies needed (at the right time and place) and that you can gain reasonable access to an online program for moving the survey online (Leedy & Omrod, 2013).

Additional considerations for technology, as previously discussed, include its value in gaining secondary data from databases already in existence such as the Database of Nursing Quality Indicators (NDNQI) and electronic health records (EHR) data. The value of technology is also noted for organizing and analyzing data such as including spreadsheets for organizing, coding, and sorting simple qualitative data or for simple descriptive and basic calculations, as previously described.

FURTHER CHALLENGES

Instrument Development

In general, it is best to avoid developing your own instrument for a clinical project, because this involves extensive education and work. If there is need for a simple survey and none exist in the area, generating questions supported in the literature or from experience can be a starting point. There are then benefits in gaining review by expert raters for ensuring the questions are correct on a brief tool developed from the literature.

Project Internal Validity

Recall from previous coursework that internal validity, or ensuring the project results are due to your intervention, is critical in making the case for your findings. You have to help ensure that alternate explanations are not the cause of your outcomes. Controlling variables helps to keep the project as tight as possible to increase confidence in your findings. At minimum, be prepared to discuss variables that may influence your findings. Further reading and consultation with your mentor are needed to address this concept.

SUMMARY

This chapter has addressed strategies for your clinical project proposal that promote confidence in the tools used and help to ensure that the resultant findings are reliable and valid. Being clear in describing project tools and protocols is key.

NEXT CHAPTER UP

After collecting data, you move to analyzing and reporting your data. Strategies for analyzing qualitative data and quantitative data are shared. An important focus will be on extending your descriptive data report to include analysis.

LEARNING ACTIVITIES

To-Do List

- Summarize your plan for data collection, including protocol/procedure in a one- to two-page abstract-type format.
- Discuss the strengths and weaknesses of your plan with your mentor. This synthesis of your ideas provides an easy communication tool for your team members.

APPENDIX 11.A: SAMPLE SURVEY FORM*

Instructions: Please circle your response to each of the following items

1. Learning skills for using an electronic health record (EHR) are important in my health care professions education.

| Strongly disagree | Disagree | Agree | Strongly agree |

I plan to use EHRs in the following ways:

2. Logging patient care

| Strongly disagree | Disagree | Agree | Strongly agree |

3. Patient progress notes

| Strongly disagree | Disagree | Agree | Strongly agree |

4. Patient billing purposes

| Strongly disagree | Disagree | Agree | Strongly agree |

5. Accessing information from other disciplines to support patient care

| Strongly disagree | Disagree | Agree | Strongly agree |

6. I do not plan to used EHRs in my practice.

| Strongly disagree | Disagree | Agree | Strongly agree |

The benefits I see to using EHRs include:

7. Help make my documentation more complete

| Strongly disagree | Disagree | Agree | Strongly agree |

8. Help me minimize errors

| Strongly disagree | Disagree | Agree | Strongly agree |

9. Help me increase my efficiency

| Strongly disagree | Disagree | Agree | Strongly agree |

10. I am adequately proficient in EHR skills.

| Strongly disagree | Disagree | Agree | Strongly agree |

Instructions: Please share your written response to the following items:

11. The challenges or problems I see to using EHRs include:

12. Where/when did you receive the most information about using EHRs in your practice?

---

* *Source:* Bonnel, 2011.

12

Writing the Data-Analysis Plans for Advanced Clinical Projects

REFLECTIVE QUESTIONS

In the last chapter you considered various issues related to collecting valid and reliable data for your proposal plans. In this chapter you will consider how best to propose plans for analyzing your data. The following reflective questions organize learning for this chapter. Which of the following do you have the most comfort with?

- Beginning to plan data reporting and analysis?
- Considering strategies and rationale for varied data-analysis methods?
- Writing the analysis plan; addressing benefits/challenges of organizing full analysis plans in the proposal?

This chapter focuses on your proposal plans for organizing/reporting and analyzing the data you collect. Strategies for analyzing subject characteristics, qualitative data, and quantitative data are shared. An important focus will be writing plans that focus on analyzing, rather than merely listing, the data obtained. As you write your proposal, this chapter also guides you in "thinking it through" or anticipating what your final report might look like.

REPORTING DATA

Advanced clinical projects consist of data, whether those data are newly generated data, synthesized from existing data, or evaluation data related to evidence being tested. Plans for both reporting and analyzing those data are important in the proposal plan. Reporting data involves relaying information, providing a description, or organizing the data that were collected. Analysis involves a detailed examination that helps you and others better understand or make sense of the data. Too often the plan for data analysis is left out or is just a mere suggestion. This plan is needed at the initial proposal stage or you are likely to end up with problems or a gap in what you wanted to convey.

In planning for both the reporting and analysis components of your proposal, remember that this analysis plan is not an afterthought, but a key component of the project purpose (back to the project triangle). To accomplish, the project plan will need to include how the collected data will be retrieved and organized. This prospective approach also helps ensure that needed data are being collected before it is time for the analysis.

For example, if your project involves surveying 30 people, each responding to 10 items, you will have to know their individual responses to items as well as the group's collective responses to items. Additionally you will have to look at individual responses across items for patterns. An easy way to gain this big picture of the data is to review the data in an Excel spreadsheet. Creating a "person by item" table allows both review of each individual's responses to survey items, to seek any patterns, as well as to look at summative average responses to each item. Paying "prospective" attention to data analysis is the focus of this chapter.

ANALYZING DATA

Organizing and reporting data is an important first step, but it is essentially just a listing of the data, or what was attained. Without showing how the data have been reviewed/considered through meaningful analysis, the numbers just become a long laundry list (i.e., long lists of community health data are not very useful unless they are organized into meaningful categories for comparisons). Analysis involves "meaning making" of the data. For example, you may report the following scores on a knowledge posttest given to community members about smoking cessation: 75, 34, 89, 52, and 61. However, those scores are meaningless unless accompanied by analysis criteria and interpretation. So what might have looked like a good, high score of 89 suddenly looks dismal when analysis guidelines indicate a total of 150 points is the possible high score and the higher the score the better.

YOUR PROPOSAL: OVERVIEW OF PLANNING FOR DATA ANALYSIS

Once your purpose statement, methods, and outcomes are identified, you then move forward with the analysis plans. These early project choices direct the analysis plans that will need to be clearly described. Planning for the data analysis involves organizing/interpreting (according to criteria) so that others understand. Approaches to data analysis include the concepts of describing and inferring. The use of qualitative and/or quantitative approaches will be guided by your project purpose and projected outcomes. The goal is to organize and plan an analysis that ties to the clinical questions addressed. Thinking through your project analysis requires anticipating what your final report might look like.

Literally every project will require some type of data analysis. For any clinical project that organizes data or evidence already available, or collects new data for evaluation of a protocol or to explore new areas, some type of data analysis is required. There are often multiple options for completing data analysis. For example, all projects will have descriptive statistics that describe sample characteristics. Depending on the project purpose/ question and methods, further data gained from this sample may then be presented as descriptive analysis or inferential analysis. Understanding the background of these approaches and why they are important is key. Sample characteristics, qualitative approaches, and quantitative approaches are further described in the following sections.

Your Proposal: Plan for Describing Sample Characteristics

Your proposal analysis plan will include an initial report of descriptive data. In almost all cases, this will include a descriptive analysis of the data collected (the interviews/surveys/observations/records reviewed). This means you will have to think ahead about how descriptive data will be shared. If you are interviewing clinicians, the characteristics you want to describe about them will have to match any demographic surveys you provide them (so you will make sure you have the correct questions on your survey to match up what you want to say about the sample). For example, if surveying clinicians, you will often want to know about their background or who are they are. What are their characteristics that are important to your clinical project? How many participated and what did they "look" like (i.e., How old were they? How long have they practiced? What are their specialties)?

While you are considering the characteristics you want to describe, it also makes sense to think ahead about how you will report this information. Think ahead about the tables you will want to share after the data are collected. Proposal completion involves detailing even to the point of building blank tables for description, including charts/boxes that hold a place for descriptive findings.

Your Proposal: Plan for Sharing Qualitative Results

If you have used a data-collection approach, such as a survey asking open-ended questions about your topic, you will have to make plans for qualitative data analysis. Your analysis plans will include review of responses to these open-ended questions and seek common themes. Themes provide a way of conveying what has been learned from long lists of word responses. It is a way to interpret and make data meaningful. In essence the goal is to learn how a topic is perceived by subjects or written about in documents (Berg, 2008).

Content analysis provides a way to gain themes from the qualitative data. In some ways it serves as a funnel, first seeking broad pictures from the data and then seeking additional patterns. It can provide a way to identify, organize, index, and retrieve data. It is asking questions of the data that relate back to the study purpose. Content analysis focuses on themes, messages, or key points in the data. Content analysis begins with:

- Reviewing raw data: listing and considering
- Organizing: creating files
- Examining/perusing: getting an overview, preliminary thoughts
- Classifying: putting data into categories/themes
- Synthesizing: generate tables, diagrams, hypothesize relationships

A theme is considered a simple phrase that captures an idea or concept. Some projects will use "a priori" coding to seek themes. This means that selected categories are named before the data are reviewed. The categories are then used in reviewing and seeing whether they are found in the data. For example, do the data responses correspond to a set criteria such as supportive or nonsupportive of a new practice policy?

Others use "open" coding. With open coding, themes emerge as common responses are heard multiple times. For example, in a qualitative survey of new charge nurses, data might reflect common concerns, or themes, about learning staffing, or engaging the team. Themes sometimes emerge as you ask what surprises me about these results.

Content Analysis Example

Using the Electronic Health Record Survey Example (Appendix 12.A), content analysis was used for open-ended question responses. For example, in completing content analysis of one specific open-ended survey question "The challenges or problems I see to using EHRs include . . . ," from the 22 responses received, the following themes were identified: issues for training, problems with access, concerns about losing data, and privacy issues. Each theme is then further described and specific examples for each category are provided.

Your Proposal: Plan for Sharing Descriptive Quantitative Results

Quantitative data analysis provides a way of summarizing your data through numbers. If quantitative data will be gained, planning choices for analysis include considering whether descriptive statistics only will be appropriate or descriptive statistics plus inferential statistics will best convey the data findings and address the project questions. For example, in planning to evaluate staff satisfaction with a specific staff development program, all responses to a specific survey item (rating 1–4 high) could be summarized according to range, mean, and standard deviation. Additionally the item scores can be averaged for a specific group and their scores reported in a similar fashion. If there is intent to compare satisfaction ratings between new staff and experienced staff, then an inferential statistic such as the *t*-test would be used to compare these two groups' mean satisfaction score (a type of inferential statistic). The analysis plan will depend on the project purpose and relates back to the project triangle.

Descriptive quantitative components are a type of counting to create a numerical picture of the data. They can include a count of contextual elements and might use, for example, tally sheets or frequency counts. These can be created by hand as one approach, but as noted, technology makes generating these counts fairly easy. Appendix 12.B and 12.C provide examples of tables using frequency counts.

Your Proposal: Inferential Quantitative Data-Analysis Plans

If you are using inferential statistics, then you analyze your data to see whether there are unique findings (showing statistical significance) or whether your findings were more probably related to chance. Inferential statistics involve meeting assumptions for inferential statistics (e.g., large sample size, usually noted to be greater than 30 to approximate a normal curve that the statistics are based on). Additionally to know you are choosing the correct inferential tests, you will need to describe the level of data in your data collection. Data-analysis tests are guided by the level of data being analyzed:

- Nominal: Data that can be put in unique categories for frequency counts. This refers to questions that ask about categories like yes/no or black/white. Modes will be reported descriptively; then further analysis with nonparametric tests such as the chi-square test can be used for category comparisons.
- Ordinal: Data that can be ordered, such as data from "good, better, best" type surveys. These data will typically be described/reported with medians/ranges; then further analysis can be used with non-parametric tests like Wilcoxon signed ranks.
- Interval/ratio: Data that can be used mathematically such as numerical scores on a knowledge test. Mean/averages and standard deviations are reported descriptively; then further analysis with parametric statistics such as t-tests, analysis of variance (ANOVA), or other tests depending on the project purpose.

Describe the Inferential Statistics to Be Used

Once you identify the level of data, return to your handy statistics text to confirm you are planning the right test for your type of data (consulting with your mentor is also a good idea). For instance, in the initial continuing-education example, it would be appropriate to compare the new and experienced staff mean satisfaction scores using an independent t-test.

A good guide for those new to advanced clinical project data-analysis plans is to select only the core variables for simple inferential testing. Again, indicate any plans to complete simple inferential tests as part of the project proposal. As you work on this section of your proposal, you will want additional readings/references to support your plans. Again if you are new to this process, a useful reference such as *Statistics for People Who Don't Think*

They Like Statistics (Salkind, 2011) can be helpful. More complex approaches to analysis can be considered with your mentor.

MAKING A PLAN FOR REPORTING THE DATA ANALYSIS: VISUAL PRESENTATION

Plan to Organize Results

Even though you have no data at the proposal stage, making plans to organize your descriptive data and data analyses provides a "step up" when it is time for the analysis. Consider the value of a large three-ring binder or its electronic equivalent. If your project will end with the traditional five scholarly sections, put five dividers in the binder at the beginning of project implementation as a reminder/placeholder for the final sections. Data-analysis plans can even include the blank table formats noted above. Although this advice is easy to ignore, it will pay dividends in saved time and frustration later.

You will want to showcase your results in the final project paper, and this often requires visualizing the project as processed and completed. Generate plans for tables or charts that can be used to document descriptive characteristics of project subjects as well as further data analyses.

Tables and charts help organize data that are too complex to just convey through paragraph form (San Francisco Edits, n.d.). Those who will read your final project paper will often find it easiest to skim your tables and charts to quickly identify findings. Creating these placeholders now for future data also provides you time to make sure you are collecting the best data to address your purpose statement. Making this plan now may even make it easier to complete the write-up of these sections as you work with these established tables (see Box 12.1).

QUICK TIPS

Sometimes it is easiest to start by sharing the descriptive data and then summarize how these data answer the project question(s). At minimum include:

- Subject demographics: Descriptive statistics are used for sharing demographic data. Share your plans for completing table or bullets with frequencies and ranges of responses for each demographic item.

BOX 12.1

Writing up the Data-Analysis Plan

This example uses a sample project on electronic health records (EHRs), having the purpose "to identify attitudes of advanced practice nursing students for using EHR documentation in their health care setting post graduation." To show evaluation plans for a 10-item quantitative survey and 2-item qualitative questions (Appendix 12.A), the following brief summary is provided.

Data analysis will be completed with basic descriptive statistics used to describe the 10 structured-response items. An Excel spreadsheet of each participant's responses will be shared (see Appendices 12.B and 12.C). This will allow for review of the numeric data for patterns. A frequency-count table will be constructed as well to further analyze subject responses with appropriate histograms generated. Qualitative responses to the two open-ended items will be typed verbatim into a word-processing program. Content analysis seeking themes will be completed by the researcher and a second health professional.

- Closed-ended (limited response) items: Descriptive statistics are used for conveying responses to survey items that are closed-ended. Share plans for completing table or bullets with frequencies and central tendency measures for each item on a survey or checklist.
- Open-ended (descriptive response) items: Common themes are gained from open-ended survey items and content analysis. Plan to share common themes identified from these items, for example, listing in bullet form or a summary table.

PLANNING AHEAD FOR PROJECT COMPLETION: DISCUSSION/IMPLICATIONS

After implementing your proposal and completing your project data analysis, you will establish conclusions and recommendations. These will be based on the synthesis of evidence from your project and your responses to your project purpose. This will help you address the "so-what?" of findings from the project.

Even in the planning phase it is important to consider potential implications. For example, plan at minimum to address further implications from the findings that relate to practice, education, and research. These implications will be related directly to your purpose statement and outcomes. For example, in the EHR survey example in this chapter, the following implications might emerge.

- For practice: Important to learn about and access EHRs as practice settings make this change.
- For education: Further education is recommended across settings.
- For further research: Further study of the best ways to learn and use EHRs is recommended.

Finally, plan to create a scholarly document to be presented that can be defended to your community of interest and present your project to stakeholders, academic communities, and interested parties.

SUMMARY

Data analysis will be a major component of your project and needs to be addressed prospectively in your proposal. This chapter provided direction for thinking ahead to final components of the project, including organizing and analyzing the data you collect. You will want to make credible plans for data analysis so that all can clearly understand your project results.

NEXT CHAPTER UP

Being ethical and accountable in your project work is a key component of clinical scholarship. Key ethical issues for project proposals will be addressed.

LEARNING ACTIVITIES

To-Do List

Review your data-analysis plans.

1. What is your level of data?
2. What are your analysis plans?
3. How do your plans flow from the purpose statement?
4. How do your analysis plans set the stage for displaying and discussing your results?
5. Does your mentor agree with your analysis?

APPENDIX 12.A: SAMPLE SURVEY FORM*

Instructions: Please circle your response to each of the following items.

1. Learning skills for using an electronic health record (EHR) are important in my health care professions education.

Strongly disagree	Disagree	Agree	Strongly agree

I plan to use EHRs in the following ways:

2. Logging patient care

Strongly disagree	Disagree	Agree	Strongly agree

3. Patient progress notes

Strongly disagree	Disagree	Agree	Strongly agree

4. Patient billing purposes

Strongly disagree	Disagree	Agree	Strongly agree

5. Accessing information from other disciplines to support patient care

Strongly disagree	Disagree	Agree	Strongly agree

6. I do not plan to use EHRs in my practice.

Strongly disagree	Disagree	Agree	Strongly agree

The benefits I see to using EHRs include:

7. Help make my documentation more complete

Strongly disagree	Disagree	Agree	Strongly agree

8. Help me minimize errors

Strongly disagree	Disagree	Agree	Strongly agree

9. Help me increase my efficiency

Strongly disagree	Disagree	Agree	Strongly agree

10. I am adequately proficient in EHR skills.

Strongly disagree	Disagree	Agree	Strongly agree

Instructions: Please share your written response to the following items:

11. The challenges or problems I see to using EHRs include:

12. Where/when did you receive the most information about using EHRs in your practice?

*Source: Bonnel, 2011.

APPENDIX 12.B: FREQUENCY COUNT, OPINIONS ABOUT ELECTRONIC HEALTH RECORDS

Number of responses for each item option from sample survey, $N = 22$.

ITEMS	D	SD	A	SA	
1.	0	1	12	9	22
2.	0	1	15	6	22
3.	0	0	13	9	22
4.	0	1	10	11	22
5.	1	0	11	10	22
6.	8	13	1	0	22
7.	0	0	14	8	22
8.	0	1	14	7	22
9.	0	1	11	10	22
10.	6	13	3	0	22

D = Disagree   A = Agree
SD = Strongly disagree   SA = Strongly agree

APPENDIX 12.C: DESCRIPTIVE RESULTS OF 22 SUBJECTS FROM SAMPLE SURVEY FORM

ITEMS	1	2	3	4	5	6	7	8	9	10
Subject 1	3	3	3	2	3	2	3	3	2	2
2	3	3	3	4	1	3	3	3	3	2
3	3	3	3	3	3	1	4	4	4	1
4	3	3	3	3	3	1	3	3	3	2
5	3	3	3	3	3	2	3	3	3	1
6	4	4	4	4	4	2	3	3	3	2
7	4	4	3	3	4	2	3	3	4	2
8	3	3	3	3	3	2	3	3	3	2
9	4	3	4	4	3	2	4	4	4	2
10	4	3	3	3	4	2	3	3	3	3
11	3	3	3	3	3	2	3	3	3	1
12	4	4	4	4	4	1	4	4	4	2
13	3	3	3	3	3	2	3	3	3	1
14	4	3	4	4	4	1	4	4	4	2
15	2	3	3	3	4	2	3	2	4	1
16	4	3	3	4	3	2	3	4	4	2
17	3	4	4	4	4	1	4	3	4	3
18	3	3	3	3	3	1	3	3	3	2
19	3	4	4	4	4	1	4	3	3	3
20	3	3	4	4	3	2	3	4	4	2
21	4	4	4	4	4	1	4	4	4	2
22	3	3	4	4	4	2	3	3	3	1

Average										
	3.30	3.27	3.41	3.45	3.36	1.68	3.31	3.27	3.41	1.86
Standard Deviation										
	0.57	0.46	0.50	0.60	0.73	0.57	0.48	0.55	0.59	0.64
Mode										
	3	3	3	4	3	2	3	3	3	2
Median										
	3	3	3	3.5	3	2	3	3	3	2

13

Keeping Clinical Projects Ethical and Dependable

The following reflective questions organize learning for this chapter. Which of the following are you most comfortable with?

- How do professional competencies and standards extend to clinical projects?
- Why is discussion of clinical project ethical issues important?
- What do these concepts mean in planning and writing a proposal?

PROFESSIONALISM AND PROFESSIONAL STANDARDS

Because you have just read about analyzing your data in the last chapter, you may feel like you are about done with your clinical project proposal. However, this is a case in which some of the most important content has been saved for last. Your project will not receive the desired recognition or acceptance you desire if it has not been conducted with the utmost integrity, and so you need to be sure that all ethical aspects of the project have been identified and addressed.

All nurses are part of the profession and are therefore required to adhere to nursing's professional values. Standards have been established by a number of professional nursing organizations to guide the implementation of those values. The American Nurses' Association's (ANA) *Scope and Standards of Practice* (2010) is one such document.

When one moves into scholarly work as with your clinical project, then additional standards and competencies apply. For example, when writing a formal paper such as the proposal, a specific writing style is identified and applied. In nursing, that is often the American Psychological Association's (APA, 2010) writing style, although other styles are also used. Ethical standards and competencies also extend to work with interprofessional teams. For example, the book *Core Competencies for Interprofessional Collaborative Practice* (Interprofessional Education Collaborative Expert Panel, 2011) has been developed and includes competency domains for values and ethics for interprofessional practice, roles and responsibilities, interprofessional communication, and teams and teamwork. Also, whenever you participate in conducting research on human subjects, the *Federal Policy for the Protection of Human Subjects* (2010) details pertinent guidelines. Using these documents can be key to completing successful professional projects.

KEY ETHICAL STANDARDS

Give Credit Where Credit Is Due

Recognizing and acknowledging the work of others is a fundamental element of scholarly writing. Whenever you use someone else's exact words, or even someone else's ideas paraphrased in your own words, you must give that person credit. Failure to recognize ideas and words that belong to someone else as his or her work, and not yours, constitutes plagiarism. Although this may seem like a simple concept, it can be deceptive. The easiest case is when you are the author of a paper (the clinical project proposal, or any paper on which you are acknowledged as the author) and you include ideas that are your own thoughts and written in your own words, and which you have never published before, then you can simply write them down and move on.

A slightly more complicated case is when you are writing your own thoughts or words, which you have previously published. In this case, and because of copyright laws, you must reference your previous thoughts or words, even though they all came from you yourself! The failure to reference your own previous work is called self-plagiarism.

A much clearer example of plagiarism is when you use or refer to someone else's ideas or words and fail to give that person credit. Credit is given by correctly referencing the source of the words or ideas, so that readers can go to that source and see the original words or ideas themselves. This practice of referencing has very important implications for your proposal. When you

- use someone else's exact words, you must insert quotation marks or italicize their words and provide the source where those exact words can be found.
- use someone else's ideas, and even if you paraphrase the ideas using your own words to describe the other person's ideas, then you must also provide the source where that exact idea can be found.
- provide the source where those words and/or ideas can be found. This must be done exactly as prescribed by the writing style you are using.

Permission to Use Instruments

Although any number of research instruments are available for use in the public domain and may be used by anyone (with appropriate referencing, of course), there are a number of instruments that do not fall in that category. Permission is required to use instruments that are unpublished and developed by someone else, as well as instruments that have been copyrighted. In both cases, you must receive formal permission to use the instruments, and that written permission must be (a) referenced in the proposal narrative and (b) provided in the appendices.

Conflict of Interest

Conflict of interest refers to researchers who do not maintain unbiased objectivity because they have something at stake or competing interests (most often, but not always, something to gain) that include some aspect(s) of the research (Steneck, 2007). Potential financial gain is frequently the first, and often the only, example of a conflict of interest that can be identified. But conflicts of interest may also include competing responsibilities or benefits of either a personal or professional nature. A clear example of conflict of interest is a company conducting research on its own product and concluding, contrary to objective analysis of the data, that it is excellent and should be widely used. Another example is when drug representatives conduct a presentation or provide gifts or meals that encourage use of their products over a competitor's, when their competitor has no chance to respond on behalf of his or her own products. A more subtle example might be a student who participates in a project with a boss or admired colleague, in which case objectivity might be lost to the advantage of the boss or colleague. Conflicts, when they exist, do not necessarily mean that the project cannot be completed. Rather, a completely honest and transparent process that identifies the conflict(s) and applies mechanisms by which objectivity can be maintained and monitored must be implemented and documented.

Human Subjects

The most comprehensive standards in any clinical project are those regarding the use of human subjects in projects and/or research (there are similarly comprehensive standards for projects that include the use of animals, although that is far less common in nursing and so is not addressed further in this book). Your own research cannot be started until these standards are met and you have written approval to begin. All researchers are expected to uphold the ethical principles of autonomy, justice, and beneficence (Steneck, 2007) through the self-regulation of their respective professions. That self-regulation is augmented by federal government legislation, which was formalized in 1974 when the Department of Health, Education and Welfare (HEW) codified the procedures of research under Title 45 of the Code of Federal Regulations, part 46 (45 CFR 46). In 1991 most federal agencies affiliated with human research adopted common regulation for human subject protections as 45 CFR 46, subpart A, which is commonly referred to as the Common Rule (*Federal Policy for the Protection of Human Subjects*, 2010).

Institutional review boards (IRBs) are established to implement and monitor the principles promulgated in the Common Rule at all institutions receiving federal dollars. Although some proposals may be deemed exempt or expedited, such classification is the IRB's purview and not the prerogative of the researchers themselves to determine. Informed consent is one of the most complex features of the Common Rule and is closely monitored by IRBs, as it is a primary mechanism by which the ethical principles of autonomy, justice, and beneficence are upheld. For example, if your project involves research components, you must inform potential participants of

- the research background, purpose, and procedures
- why they have been asked to participate

- their right to not participate, without any negative repercussions
- their right to withdraw from the study at any time without negative repercussions
- their right to ask questions about participation
- their right to voluntarily consent to participation without coercion
- their right to know the benefits of participating, as well as any risks or inconveniences
- their right to confidentiality
- access to the researcher's contact information in case they have questions or are injured

With this information, and being as fully informed as possible, potential participants are able to make autonomous decisions about their willingness to participate in a project or not.

If your project will require a consent form, many organizations provide consent-form templates for project directors. Go to your own institution's website and see whether you can find an example (Box 13.1). If you do not find a template at your own organization, or if you want to compare templates, an example is provided on the University of Missouri–Kansas City's website: http://www.umkc.edu/umkc-search/?cx=0082816574086 03500330%3Avpif2cmpa14&cof=FORID%3A10&ie=UTF-8&q=sample%20 consent%20forms

The implications of the Common Rule are far reaching for all students and researchers conducting clinical projects with human subjects. The good news is that you only need to know that virtually all research involving human subjects must be submitted to, reviewed by, and approved in writing by the IRB before it is implemented. But this IRB review process takes time, and so you need to account for that in your projected project timeline. Also, although the Common Rule provides the guidelines, each institution has its own specific policies and procedures on how the Common Rule is implemented, and so it is your responsibility to know the policies and procedures for your own institution. Keep in mind, too, that if you are associated with multiple institutions and/or will conduct the project at multiple sites, all of those sites/institutions must review the proposal and provide written approval. Caution: No aspect of the project may be started until written approval from the IRB is received.

Data Integrity

You are nearing completion of your project proposal, and you already have a wealth of time and effort invested. It is imperative that you take the time and steps necessary now to ensure the dependability of the data when you

> ### BOX 13.1
>
> **Agency Website**
>
> Go to your institution(s)'s website and see what policies and procedures exist with relevance to your project proposal. Keep in mind that if you hold multiple roles (such as student and employee), or if you will use multiple project sites, you must comply with all involved institutions.

are done because, without that, the reputation and impact of your hard work will not be respected by the scientific community and practicing nurses.

You have already anticipated and addressed several threats to dependable and reliable, or trustworthy and transferable, data during the design and data-collection procedures of your project. For example, you chose reliable instruments, and/or you decided to use triangulation approaches. Now you must also ensure the integrity of the data through ongoing, accurate, confidential, and dependable record keeping. This process is often facilitated by an ongoing log of your daily activities and decisions, as is captured in an audit trail.

FINAL STEPS

There are lots of ethical aspects to research and other scholarly work. The best advice is to be well informed on the ethical issues and to address them up front, during the proposal phase of your clinical project. Remember to consult with project mentors on any questions. This is not an area where it is best to "ask for forgiveness afterward," so be proactive and transparent in your preparations. Go through the entire list of ethical aspects, be absolutely honest with yourself and your team, and address each item now.

NEXT CHAPTER UP

You now have a fairly complete proposal in hand, and you have addressed the ethical elements and ramifications of the project as well. Your next step is to edit, revise, and finalize the proposal so that it is ready for others to review.

As you revise and edit, you will be laying the groundwork for your final project paper, and that will (hopefully) have widespread distribution, even publication, and you want everything to be accurate as well as conducive to finishing that final report/paper.

LEARNING ACTIVITIES

To-Do List

If your project will require consent forms, use your agency's template to start a draft of your consent form, being sure to include:

- the name of the study and researchers
- why any individuals are being asked to participate
- brief rationale for study and participation
- brief explanation of study purpose
  - brief explanation of the study procedures and the nature of the participant's activities and time commitment
- the benefits (including any payment/compensation)
- risks of participation (including fees)
  - that participation is voluntary, with no negative consequences if they choose not to participate, as well as alternatives to participation
- individuals may withdraw at any time, without negative consequences
- confidentiality
- who to contact if they have questions/problems/injury
- signature block for participant and consenter

14

Finalizing the Proposal as Professional Document: Reviewing, Editing, and Revising

REFLECTIVE QUESTIONS

The following reflective questions organize learning for this chapter. Which of the following do you have the most comfort with?

- Finalizing the proposal draft (including edits/revisions) as a professional document?
- Considering next steps in using the proposal for moving toward project completion?
- Optimizing use of self-assessment and the project team to finalize the proposal?

As you finalize your proposal you are striving to become precise in your language and making sure your readers understand clearly what you mean. As clinicians advance their education and their standing in the health care arena, professional written communication will be key. Project proposals have applications in many arenas and underscore the value of this professional document. Previous chapters have focused on the content to include in a proposal. This chapter finalizes planning for the professional document. It involves tailoring the writing to the professional audience. It also includes continuing the ideas/plans into the next phases of implementing the project and thinking ahead to how the project results and discussion will be conveyed.

EDITING/REVISING THE FIRST DRAFT

Clear communication is central in scholarly work. Often people write out plans they think are perfectly clear but then realize the information is only clear to them (of course they already know what they are doing—now clarifying the wording so others understand is key). Although the initial drafts are a matter of "getting it down" and making it clear to yourself, the final draft is about making written communication clear to others. This means reflecting on the current draft (what has been produced or written?) and what still needs to be done to finalize the proposal. It includes the use of precise language and staying consistent with terms to make sure your reader can understand and easily follow your meaning. Communication models support sending clear messages that others can interpret and respond to via feedback.

COMPLETING THE FINAL PROPOSAL

The hallmark of completing the proposal is paying attention to all of the details, including the proposal substance, structure, appendices, and writing/editing. Suggested questions to guide this process follow.

QUESTIONS TO GUIDE YOU IN DETAILING THE PROPOSAL

Proposal Substance

Conveying important content that helps enhance your project proposal is key. Make sure you have addressed the following:

- Is the project purpose important in helping care for or benefit your population of interest?
- Is the proposal purpose statement clearly written and consistently re-stated throughout the proposal?

- Are the three triangle anchors—purpose, methods, and outcomes—consistent throughout the proposal?
- Have summaries been used to repeat key section ideas for reader clarity?

Proposal Structure

Writing a proposal that meets scholarly criteria for communicating with other professionals is key. Are the following proposal sections clearly identified and written in scholarly format?

- Introductory section clarifying the project problem and purpose
- Review of the literature
- Methods section

Proposal Appendices

The appendices must be complete, and referred to in the narrative. Do they include:

- The data-collection tools?
- Agency agreements to complete the project?
- Needed human subjects approvals?
- Any consent forms (approved)?

Writing/Editing

First, self-edit using at minimum the following basic guides.

- Has the approved writing style (such as the American Psychological Association [APA]) been used correctly and consistently?
- Has clear wording been used?
- Have consistent tenses been used throughout?
- Have terms and abbreviations been appropriately introduced and referred to consistently throughout?
- Have headings been used to their best advantage to help outline the content and facilitate smooth flow of content? These headings

link the proposal parts together, provide cues for the reader, and keep the reader moving forward.
- Has all cited work been referenced appropriately?

FURTHER WRITING TIPS

Staying clear with your message is key. Further tips for clarifying your written proposal include the following.

- Avoid Excessive Use of Abbreviations and Avoid Confusing Abbreviations: For example, if you are referring to mental illness as "MI," medical–surgical nurses will immediately think about myocardial infarction. Again, be sure all abbreviations are properly introduced per your respective writing-style guidelines.
- Use Appropriate Terms Appropriately (Do Not Mix Concepts): Define the terms you will be using in initial sections of the proposal. For example, "simulation" is sometimes used to indicate standardized patients and other times to describe high-fidelity technology-supported simulation. Be clear about what you mean.
- Stay Consistent With Key Terms: Do a final "search" on the main terms (and any that you have described as interchangeable) and make sure they are consistent in all sections of the proposal. Go back and see what terms you used early on and confirm consistent use throughout the proposal.
- Use Summary Statements: Summary statements can be powerful in tying parts of a proposal together.
- Use Scholarly Language; Be Precise in Methods Language: Especially for similar-sounding terms, be careful to use the right term. For example, do not mix up the terms "content validity" and "content analysis."
- Seek Consistency in Lists: Lists of items should include consistent phrasing for each item in the list. For example, if the first item is stated with the "ing" phrase, then all successive items on the list should be stated in the same way (i.e., caring, coupling, and changing).
- Punctuate: Make sure that sentences are not too long and hard to follow. Can you read each sentence aloud and still breathe at the end?

- Keep Paragraph Lengths Appropriate: Avoid creating a page full of sentences or "wall of words" that is hard to follow. One strategy to address this is to be sure you use appropriate paragraph lengths.
- Write Using the Recommended Style: Although there are a variety of writing styles and you should use whatever you have been directed to follow, APA is often used in nursing. The writing guidelines will direct all aspects of your final written proposal. For example, APA uses the third-person format (the typical scholarly format). If first person is preferred, check first with your reviewing source/agency.
- Read the Full Project Draft: This helps you gain the big picture; you can then focus on needed details (Galvan, 2006).

FINALIZING THE TIMELINE AND PROJECT BUDGET

If not previously addressed in the proposal, now is the time to consider the project timeline and budget. These are two valuable components that keep a project moving forward.

What Is the Project Timeline?

While you have been thinking tentatively about a timeline for your project, this is the time to finalize it. As you return to your project map, consider what needs to happen when. List out each component of the proposal requiring an action and generate a best estimate of a time frame. One of the benefits of Word tables or Excel spreadsheets such as Gantt charts is that they help you stay on track and communicate your plan clearly to others.

What Is the Project Budget?

While you have been thinking tentatively about a budget for your project proposal, this is the time to finalize that essential element. Some clinical projects will have minimal budgets that will be subsumed as part of the work contribution to a setting. Sometimes there will be costs such as preparing surveys and/or providing snacks for participants. Consider and note these items.

If the proposal is for some type of grant funding, the project budget will be large enough to require a specific budget and budget justification. Excel spreadsheets can assist in clearly documenting and justifying the budget.

NEXT STEPS FOR THE PROPOSAL

To help you keep on track for implementing and completing your project proposal, now is the time to give thought to your project completion and final analysis and write-up. This will involve attending to sections of your final project write-up, including planning for the sections on Results, Discussion, and Implications.

Planning for the Results Section

How will you describe the results you gain from data collection? Remember to build in paragraphs that convey plans for completing sections four and five, the results of the project and the discussion of the findings. However you are collecting data—from interviews, surveys, observations, or document reviews—you will want to organize your information in a logical and accessible format for your readers. A review of basic considerations includes the following examples of varied project types.

- Planning for the write-up of evidence-generating projects. If you have implemented an evidence-generating project, such as interviews or surveys, your results will include a description of these project outcomes.
- Planning for the write-up of evidence-based implementation and evaluation projects. For example, if you have implemented a change project or quality-improvement project, your results will include a description of your evaluation of these projects.
- Planning for the write-up of an evidence-synthesizing project. You will plan to summarize the outcomes from your systematic literature review. This will include a description of your specific approach to the review, critique of your literature, and overall summary of strengths and weaknesses of the evidence. For some projects this will include a product that is a protocol or outline for a journal article.

As noted earlier, this is the time to lay out sample blank tables to await your data and analyses. Consider organizing your qualitative data in a spreadsheet or table format for analysis. Quantitative data can be prepared in table format for descriptive results and then further statistical tests reported. Earlier chapters provide further discussion on analysis plans.

Planning for the Discussion Section

The discussion section serves as a type of commentary. It provides opportunity to share your interpretation and opinions about your project findings as well as discuss the implications of your findings. Also you will address: What was accomplished by doing your project? And what was gained from learning the specific results? The discussion should also suggest to the reader what action should be taken and what should be done given these findings. Approaches include tying results to the initial review of the literature; relating your findings to the project purpose/questions; implications or "so what" of your findings; and strengths and limitations.

Relating Your Findings to the Project Purpose

Relating your findings back to your purpose statement helps keep your findings focused. You also have the opportunity to relate project findings or outcomes to your initial theories and hypotheses.

Tying Results to the Initial Literature Review

As noted, again plan to consider the literature and describe the similarities or differences found. Your initial literature review fits your project into the context of the literature. Now it is time to put your project findings into the literature-review context. Show that your findings fit into the literature.

Identifying Implications of Your Findings

The "so what" approach to findings includes addressing further implications for education, practice, and further research. This includes implications for your populations, patients, staff, and students.

Anticipating the Project Strengths/Limits

Remind yourself to reconsider the strengths/limits of your planned project at this point and document these. Sample description of limits for a small project might include:

> *Limits*: Small descriptive sample results; tested in only one setting.
> *Strengths*: Protocol developed from best-evidence literature; expert peer-review panel for protocol review.

USING THE ABSTRACT AS A TOOL TO FINALIZE

The abstract will be the most read and beneficial document of your project, stating clearly in limited space what was done, why it was done, when the project was finished, and the outcomes and implications. Your abstract will include the key components of your proposal in abbreviated form. It can serve as a checklist that all important components have been addressed. This abbreviated format also provides an easy communication tool for your team members. Box 14.1 provides an example of an abstract.

When you finalize your project, the proposal abstract will be revisited with an opportunity to fill in any data "blanks." You will take your initial abstract and revise to show that work has been completed. Additionally, you will highlight project results and implications of these results. Broadly your abstract answers these questions:

- Why did you begin the project?
- What specifically did you do?
- What did you learn?
- What are the implications?

BOX 14.1

Sample Abstract Using Glucose Patterns to Improve Diabetes Management in Long-Term Care

The long-term-care (LTC) setting often provides systems-level challenges for both facility nurses and primary care providers who manage residents with diabetes. The purpose of this project is to outline the development of a diabetes management module that can be used as a facilitated training resource by staff nurses working in LTC, and to describe the impact of this intervention at the systems level. A 151-bed nursing care facility in the Midwest region of the United States is the site for a quality-improvement project to educate 10 facility nurses on evidence-based practices for interpreting plasma glucose data, identifying trends and patterns, and communicating findings to providers. An instructional module was developed and piloted with nurse-managers and staff nurses at the facility. A pre/posttest and module evaluation survey demonstrated positive acquisition of knowledge and skills related to content at the time of implementation. A guided discussion session evaluated the sustainability of this intervention on individual clinical behaviors and the effect at the systems level. Through enhanced awareness and partnership with facility nurses, nurse practitioners will be better able to access and act on information essential to the improvement of glucose control for residents with diabetes—Roberta Mansfield (2010).

To convert these questions into a scholarly communication format, the scholarly parts addressed in the abstract should include:

- *Background*: Why was this important? What was your purpose in doing this?
- *Brief literature*: What evidence did you find for the need/approach?
- *Methods*: What did you do? (systematic description) How did you analyze/evaluate?
- *Results*: Placeholder for the outcomes you will gain.
- *Implications*: Placeholder for discussing why the findings are important to your populations as well as implications for education, practice, and research.

TOOLS THAT FACILITATE PROPOSAL COMPLETION

The Project Team/Committee

Recall that you have developed a team or committee to support you through the clinical project process. Just as the patient is part of his or her own clinical team, you are an important part of your project team/committee. Once you have thoroughly reviewed and edited the proposal, seek your team or committee's review and use their time wisely.

Peer Review

Peer or colleague review of your proposal can be complementary to team and mentor reviews. Seeking input and feedback from others who work with similar situations or topics can be invaluable; this offers another objective review. The review provides an opportunity for further dialogue and further questions. If you serve as a peer reviewer, remember your role includes providing feedback that gives direction as well as offering encouragement and support to your colleague. Benefits of providing peer review include gaining critical-appraisal skills, participating in an interactive process, and practice at providing constructive feedback (Boehm & Bonnel, 2010).

With the opportunity of gaining peer or mentor feedback also comes the responsibility of receiving constructive feedback, reflecting, and responding to that feedback (Leedy & Omrod, 2013). For example, working with mentors in finishing the proposal involves clear communication and response to feedback on schedule. It also includes being mindful and respectful in use of others' time.

Self-Review and Your Decision Trail

Reflection can provide a review or debriefing of project experiences. Reflection allows you to make explicit what you are doing and learning. Opportunities are gained to focus and facilitate project learning and promote quality improvement for future projects.

As you continue your reflective writing and decision trail, remember to write about what you are doing, what barriers you have, how you deal with these, and general thoughts/impressions about how the project is progressing. Make an effort to extend this experience to a weekly reflection on your project. The value of the ongoing reflections includes serving as a written reflection to help document project process and analysis. They can be written to help you record thoughts on the implementation process as well as emerging data. This writing can be helpful when you complete your final project write-up.

REFLECTING AND SELF-EDITING

As you read your final proposal draft out loud, are these concepts, described earlier in your work, evident?

1. Does the challenge/problem grab and convince within the first page?
2. Are precise, consistent words used to describe key concepts?
3. Are unnecessary adjectives deleted such as "extra-special?"
4. Is the "third person" maintained throughout (or first person if acceptable via guidelines)?
5. Are perfected grammar and spelling in place?
6. Are abbreviations used only minimally, if at all?

Your Own Accountability

As you move forward with your clinical project, you will continue to exercise and strengthen skills that have helped you get to this point. Assets such as accountability and goal setting will serve you well in finalizing your proposal and moving to the implementation phase of your clinical project. Tools to help in being accountable and to further goal setting:

- Avoid the blame game
- Ask relevant questions and use feedback
- Work at problem solving

- Recognize strengths and limitations of a project
- Continue your decision/audit trail

TURNING THE PROPOSAL INTO A FINISHED PROJECT DOCUMENT

An important goal for the proposal is that it be used as the basis for a completed project. In most cases this involves using the initial sections of the proposal as they stand; the methods section of your proposal is then revised to document completion, meaning verbage is changed to past tense and any clarifying details of the actual project implementation are added. Results and implications sections, sections 4 and 5, as noted previously are then completed.

SUMMARY

Clear communication is central in scholarly work. Completing the proposal involves gaining better writing skills, not only planning project methods, but clearly conveying them. The value of gaining new tools for writing/completing the clinical project proposal and reflecting on what has been accomplished is a part of this. Considering next steps in implementing the proposal helps move toward project completion and contributes to quality patient care outcomes.

NEXT CHAPTER UP

How do you move forward with your proposal-implementation plans? What next steps exist for using your proposal? The next chapter helps you address these questions.

LEARNING ACTIVITIES

To-Do List

A final check:

1. Is the full document packaged professionally as a scholarly document? Does it follow a systematic approach? Appropriate metrics?

Reasonable analysis plans? Do you have plans for tables and graphs, to clearly convey future findings?

2. Has your proposal been peer reviewed (by colleagues, mentor, project team)?

3. Have you written summaries of each proposal section for clarity? Is the finished proposal in scholarly written format?

15

Keeping Your Advanced Clinical Project Proposal Going

REFLECTIVE QUESTIONS

In the last chapter you considered the importance of finalizing your written proposal. The following reflective questions guide this chapter. Which of the following do you have the most comfort with?

- Reflecting on what's been gained?
- Considering next steps in implementing and evaluating the proposal?
- Considering next steps in completing and sharing the completed proposal project?

This chapter is about pulling the entire project together. It allows you the opportunity to stop and celebrate the accomplishment of a well-written proposal. It encourages reflecting on the big picture of what has been learned in developing this proposal and reflecting on what still needs to be done.

The advanced clinical project has helped you name and focus your area of expertise. This chapter brings full circle to creating proposals for projects that enhance safe, quality patient care for diverse populations and settings. Using best practices in mentoring, peer review, and self-assessment will help achieve these objectives. Additional focus on how best to incorporate technology and interprofessional education (IPE) is addressed. Implementing the proposal and completing the project then lead to opportunities for further sharing/disseminating and further projects. The proposal will be used as a component of a final paper reporting on your complete project.

THE PROPOSAL: REFLECTING ON WHAT HAS BEEN GAINED

Clinical Scholarship Models

The clinical project proposal provides an opportunity to extend scholarship to the clinical setting. The Boyer (1990) model focuses on scholarship in four broad domains; clinical projects often relate to the scholarship of application. Boyer describes the scholarship of application as applying knowledge from theory, practice, and research to address goals related to client outcomes, community concerns, and environmental challenges.

The American Association of Colleges of Nursing (AACN; 2006) in its Doctorate of Nursing Practice Essentials discusses forms of scholarship as including the clinical project. Through gaining proposal skills, you have gained skills such as those described in the doctorate of nursing practice (DNP) graduate competencies, including methods to:

- Review and synthesize the best evidence for practice
- Develop projects to evaluate practice at varied levels from patient to populations and systems
- Use quality-improvement tools to enhance practice
- Use best evidence to guide protocol development to enhance patient care
- Use technology to gain data to better understand patient care process and outcomes and generate further projects

Health Professions Education Guides

Guidelines relevant to Health Professions Education include the Quality and Safety Education for Nurses program (Cronenwett et al., 2009) and the Institute of Medicine (2003). These also relate to the AACN (2006) guides for clinical scholarship and suggest direction for future project proposals.

- *Evidence-based practice*: The focus on evidence has been emphasized throughout this text. Reflect on how your proposal will help extend the use of evidence in practice. Consistent with guides for

DNP scholarship (AACN, 2006), this is central to the work of all advanced practice nurses.

- *Enhancing use of technology*: Rapid advances in electronic health records and various clinical databases provide new opportunities for gaining data to better understand patient populations and their needs as well as to document outcomes. Opportunities to gain data via provider, patient, and technology interfaces offer opportunities to advance scholarship. Using technology to its fullest potential can include creative use of newer technologies that facilitate both staff and patient interventions and data collection.
- *Enhancing collaborative work*: Optimizing the use of interprofessional teams is a central component of the agenda to improve health care. Teamwork included in team-supported clinical projects is an essential component of patient-centered care. Recently, interprofessional competencies that include clear communication and scholarship have been developed to help move this effort forward (Interprofessional Education Collaborative, 2011).
- *Quality improvement*: The essence of advanced clinical projects is improving quality care. Clinical projects have the potential to lead to changes in systems and enhance quality and safety. In today's data-driven world, scholarly skills gained in proposal writing and project completion are key components for future lifelong learning and evidence-based practice.
- *Patient-centered care*: Opportunities to gain the patients' perspective in what is meant by quality care. Focus on safety is a key component of relevant clinical projects as well.

NEXT STEPS: USING THE PROPOSAL

Although this book is about proposal writing, providing a "hint" to the next project phases is appropriate. Next steps involve project implementation/evaluation, writing the final report, and continuing scholarly plans.

Implementing/Evaluating

As you think forward to the next steps of your project, major components include adhering to project protocols, continuing team communication, and working professionally with any team members.

Adhering to Project Protocols as You Implement and Evaluate Your Proposal

At this point, you have laid out your plans; hence, all involved know what is going on. Now it is your responsibility to stay true to your plans. In large part, this has included clear documentation about approved project plans/ processes. If unforeseen challenges should occur, you need to communicate with your team about any needed protocol changes and to confirm any alternate plans.

Another way to document that you are staying true to your plans is achieved in part by keeping decision or audit trails. These tools also serve as timelines and journals of not only what is being done but also why choices are being made.

Continuing Communication and Working Professionally With Team Members

The proposal is the contract with a project committee or other team members. It provides the detail for keeping others on track (clarifying who will do what, and when). Implementation also involves meeting professional standards in working with the team, the project setting, and participants. Clinical project teamwork may include direct involvement with patients, working with staff to enhance protocols/approaches, or working with larger unit/system approaches to enhance safe/quality patient care. As a clinical leader you will have opportunities to guide staff in evidence-based projects. You will want a proposal that is clear and concise to share with the team: to be able to convey your plan to help document clinical outcomes and to improve structure/process as needed.

NEXT STEPS: FINAL REPORT WRITE-UP

Your proposal will become part of the early sections of your final paper, in which you report on your completed project. The final sections in scholarly documents are the results and then discussion/implications section. As noted previously, the results section of a paper is considered "just the facts." It is a detailing of the data that was gained in an organized meaningful presentation of what was learned. The fifth section of the traditional scholarly paper includes the discussion/implications information. In this section, the findings are considered from the "so what" perspective. In other words, what do these findings mean? Your well-written proposal can lead to a strong finished project with potential benefits to safe, quality patient care.

NEXT STEPS: ADVANCING WITH CONTINUED CLINICAL SCHOLARSHIP

The importance of supporting lifelong learning for all health professionals has been acknowledged (Institute of Medicine, 2011). This includes ongoing learning by proposing and completing clinical projects; such scholarly projects can become a key part of learning. Recall that the project proposal is also a tool to prepare for future work in advanced clinical leadership. Clinical project proposal writing serves as a bridge to advanced clinical leadership. Project proposals can lead to:

- Future presentations/publications
- Proposals for future grant writing
- Opportunities for further clinical projects

The Value of the Portfolio in Further Project Write-Up

A reflective portfolio that documents your proposal journey can be a major tool in furthering your project scholarship. A portfolio that documents each of the sections of your proposal can showcase your ongoing clinical project progress and document one component of your clinical expertise. The benefits of portfolios include helping document/track components with other team members and sharing with others the scholarship that is developed in a clinical setting.

Portfolios serve as a way to share your story about purposes and strategies for projects that advance safe, quality patient care. They also serve as a way to document clinical scholarship via naming/describing knowledge gained and support generation of questions that require further study. The portfolio is a tool to promote reflection and communication about accomplishments. A portfolio of your proposal, and later your project, helps support:

- Reflection on what you do
- Communication with others about what you do
- Ownership of the work and learning that has been accomplished

- Value in helping document this lengthy project
- Organization for further project scholarship

Completing the Project and Planning for Publication

Scholarship models include dissemination of scholarly work. According to Huber and Hutchings (2005), projects must be peer reviewed and passed on via public venues such as publications. Oermann and Hays (2011) summarize reasons to publish include: sharing expertise, disseminating new evidence, gaining advancement (in both education and clinical settings), developing your own knowledge and skills, and achieving your own satisfaction. Those in diverse advanced clinician roles in particular have reason to write to share knowledge gained related to improving patient care. Just as in proposal writing, revising a final project to suit publication format will include building a timeline for planning, selecting the appropriate journal, and writing according to the journal's guidelines.

Proposals for Future Grant Writing

As advanced clinicians there will be opportunity to write proposals and gain resources to document scholarship with populations of interest. In learning proposal-writing skills, you have additionally gained tools for critiquing and synthesizing the literature, created worksheets for laying out the big-picture plans, and created templates for mapping out future projects. Concepts used in proposal writing and in creating sections of proposals apply across all scholarly venues. These tools serve to make the case for future projects. The potential for grant funding exists with well-written proposals.

Proposals for Further Clinical Projects

The initial project proposal often serves as a tool for reflecting and learning as the basis to generate further projects. In considering future plans, recall that project proposals help communicate about what you do as an advanced clinician and address further goal setting or "what's next?" with your specialty. The project may lead to using project methods in further venues and to extending expertise with your specialty population. Advanced clinicians have opportunities to practice with unique populations. These projects can help others better understand these populations and serve as tools for mentoring others.

ADDITIONAL CONCEPTS OF VALUE

Continuing the Mentor Partnership

Throughout the development of your proposal/project, you have been working with a mentor of some type. As noted, related to the mentoring process, the best use of resources is to find a mentor whose interests already match yours or are closely related. This provides a type of incentive for all to eagerly move forward. It also involves fair, equitable use of both mentor and mentee time.

In most cases, you will stay connected with faculty mentors after the proposal is completed. You may consider renegotiating for future work. Other possibilities include moving on to another mentor or considering whether you are ready to take on the mentoring role yourself.

Caring for Self and Having a Peer Group

Staying motivated to complete a big project involves caring for oneself. Remember to create time and space to care for yourself as well as focusing on your scholarship. This includes creating time and activities for physical and emotional health as well. Colleague or peer groups can play a role as well. Peers can help in debriefing project activities and help you stay motivated to complete your project as well. Peer groups can be formalized to include scheduled journal club-type activities or be maintained in informal venues.

CONTINUING SELF-ASSESSMENT AND REFLECTION

Scholarship and mindful clinical practice go hand in hand. You have reflected as you completed the proposal; learning through reflection and reflecting on learning will enhance future work. Using reflective journaling has been a key concept in your proposal writing. At each stage of proposal writing, as you have made choices that further directed your work, you have addressed the basic questions of what, so what, now what? Now as you finish your proposal, reflecting on the full process and product provides opportunities to cement learning and gain a basis for future ideas and plans. Here are some reflective prompts to guide thoughts on your proposal work:

1. Why was this work important to you?
2. What was the most important thing that you learned from creating this proposal?

3. How does this proposal help you document what you do as an advanced clinician?
4. What was it like for you to create this proposal? What most surprised you about your work on this proposal?
5. What did you gain from creating this proposal? What new skills or strategies were acquired?
6. How did this proposal work expand your previous knowledge? How did this advance your thinking about the topic or subject area?
7. How did this work enhance your role as an advanced clinician?
8. How will you be able to use what you gained from this experience in future work as an advanced clinician?
9. If you were to continue your work on this product, what further approaches would you consider?
10. What further learning goals do you have related to this work?

FINAL SUMMARY

Proposal-writing skills are important for nurses to develop. You have created a proposal for a project of interest. Whether administrative, clinical, staff developmental, or other, your proposal has been guided by the best evidence available as you considered the theories and models available. Your blend of knowledge, motivation, and the setting of your research will likely lead to further work as you implement, finalize, and then share your project with others.

Being an expert clinician comes with the responsibility of scholarship. Once the proposal is implemented, the opportunity exists to further package and disseminate your learning. Gaining tools for scholarly writing provides the beginning of your journey. Creating a portfolio showcasing the entire project helps package and lay the groundwork for further presentation/publication. Good proposals can lead to good projects. Results of these important clinical projects then lead to developing practice improvements and helping to direct the future of patient care.

Appendices

A

Project Triangle Model

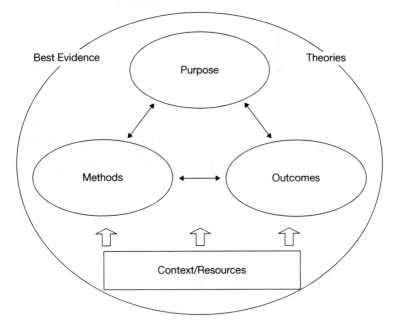

Once you have clearly identified the project problem, you are ready to use components of this model to develop your proposal. The Rubric in Appendix B will assist you in reflecting on your work.

B

Rubric for Planning or Self-Assessment of a Specific Project

As you move forward with your project proposal, check to see whether you have adequately addressed each of the following. Note "agree" or "disagree" to confirm that each area has been thoroughly considered.

Concept	Have You Considered	Agree/Disagree
Evidence-based practice	What evidence is available to guide initiating and implementing a particular project?	
Theory or conceptual model	What theories might best fit in guiding the project?	
Logistics/context with assessment of unit/setting	Have you assessed feasibility of your project? What are the facilitators/barriers for completing the project in a specific setting?	
Purpose	Does the purpose flow from the identified problem? What is to be achieved with the project?	
Methods	What is the best approach for your given problem and project purpose?	
Outcomes evaluation	What are your project outcomes to be evaluated? How will you know your project is successful?	
Reflective review/critique	What are the strengths and weaknesses of your proposal? Are there points you can strengthen?	

C

Evidence Synthesis: Anesthesia Considerations and Implications for Obese Pediatric Patients

PROPOSAL ABSTRACT – KARRI ARNDT

The number of Americans described as being overweight or obese has been increasing at an alarming rate over the past 30 years. Overweight and obesity in both children and adults have been identified not only by the United States Department of Health and Human Services, Centers for Disease Control (2009) as an epidemic in the United States but also by the World Health Organization (WHO) as a pandemic (2009). The WHO (2009) states that childhood obesity is one of the most serious public health challenges of the 21st century. As the rate of overweight and obese individuals increases, so does the economic burden of obesity-related health care in the United States and worldwide.

Many diseases that were once thought to be present only in adults are now being seen in children and teenagers. These include cardiovascular disease, hypertension, elevated cholesterol levels, diabetes, insulin resistance, metabolic syndrome, musculoskeletal disorders, osteoarthritis, certain types of cancers, and sleep apnea. Concerns specific to anesthesia include obstructive sleep apnea, difficult mask ventilation, difficult intubation, and asthma. These comorbid conditions are known to increase the risk associated with anesthesia and are a growing concern among pediatric anesthesia providers.

Ambulatory surgery centers are also seeing a greater number of obese pediatric patients in their facilities for what are typically considered minor to moderate outpatient procedures. However, the presence of these comorbid conditions is making safe care a challenge in these facilities as anesthesia providers do not have the same ancillary resources, invasive equipment, difficult airway devices, or various medical services readily available in the event of a complication or emergency. These facilities also are not equipped for overnight stays should perioperative complications arise. It is imperative that anesthesia providers have a thorough understanding of the anesthetic implications and unique challenges associated with the obese pediatric population.

The purpose of this project is to review the current literature related to perioperative morbidity, mortality, issues, and concerns that arise when caring for obese pediatric patients requiring anesthesia services to prepare an educational article for submission to the American Association of Nurse Anesthetists (AANA) professional journal for publication.

A comprehensive review article using the most current evidence-based data will describe the prevalence of obesity in children, identify coexisting diseases and their management, discuss pharmacokinetic and pharmacodynamic considerations, identify anesthetic management techniques for this unique patient population, and identify specific questions that require further research. The purpose of the article will be to increase awareness of pediatric obesity and its implications and improve knowledge and competency of anesthesia providers, which will better prepare them to safely handle increasing numbers of obese children, especially in the ambulatory setting. More specific research is needed in this area, and an article of this nature is intended to stimulate thought, provoke questions, and motivate providers to initiate such research and disseminate their findings to improve perioperative management of this complex patient population.

METHODOLOGY

The methodology for collecting data and information for this project will include an exhaustive review of the literature located in PubMed, CINAHL, ProQuest, the Cochrane Library, and Google Scholar using the key words *pediatric, obesity, anesthesia, morbidity,* and *mortality.* Other sources to be searched include the American Society of Anesthesiologists, the AANA, the Society for Pediatric Anesthesia, and current anesthesia text and reference books, using the same key-word searches. The Centers for Disease Control will be searched for current statistical data related to the prevalence of and trends in childhood obesity.

Information obtained from the database searches will be reviewed and critically assessed for relevance and reliability. References in high-quality studies will also be reviewed for potential relevant material. Obtained data will then be organized in an easy-to-review database matrix that will identify the reference citation, type of article or research conducted, evidence obtained, key points, and limitations. Information will then be combined into a concise review article according to the guidelines set forth by the AANA (n.d.) for submission of manuscripts. The manuscript will include an introduction, history and review of literature section, discussion of state-of-the-art information, a summary of the anesthetic implications associated with the perioperative care of obese pediatric patients, and recommendations for future research. The manuscript will undergo peer and capstone committee reviews for clarity and accuracy. The peer review will include practicing certified registered nurse anesthetists and anesthesiologists who routinely work with pediatric patients.

D

Evidence Implementing and Testing: Improving the Communication of Clinical Information Between Nurses and Physicians in Long-Term Care

PROPOSAL ABSTRACT – LINDA KROEGER

Based on personal observation, experience in receiving calls from long-term-care (LTC) facilities, and conversations with physicians, registered nurses (RNs), and licensed practical nurses (LPNs) who expressed frustration with their phone interactions, a brief needs assessment was done regarding nurse/provider calls to and from LTC facilities. Several LPNs reported that their biggest fear was calling to speak with a physician regarding a change in a patient's condition because they lacked confidence in their ability to answer questions asked by the physician.

PURPOSE

The purpose of this quality-improvement project is to use developed methods, established protocols, and structured communication techniques to develop and implement a program to teach LTC nurses, including RNs and LPNs, how to efficiently and competently collect and communicate clinical information to physicians.

SETTING

A request for participation in this quality-improvement project will be made to the director of nursing of a local nursing home. The nursing home consists of six units; each unit has 16 beds and the facility capacity is 96 residents. The facility provides long-term residential care and skilled-nursing care.

SAMPLE

The nursing staff at this LTC facility is composed of RNs and LPNs. RNs include the director of nursing, the assistant director of nursing, and two Minimum Data Set nurses.

An RN and two LPNs staff the LTC unit on the day and evening shift, and two LPNs are responsible for the night shift. The nursing home also has nurses who work on call and other LPNs available. The number of RNs and LPNs who will be invited to participate in this quality-improvement (QI) program for communication training is approximately 13.

QUALITY-IMPROVEMENT PLAN

The training program for communication techniques will begin with an introduction on organizational tips to consider before calling the physician. This will be followed by instruction on the use of the Situation, Background, Assessment, Recommendation (SBAR) communication technique. The SBAR method has the support of the Institute for Healthcare Improvement and The Joint Commission. SBAR is an established, evidence-based method shown to be effective in improving clinical communication skills (American Medical Directors Association [AMDA], 2009; Dunsford, 2009). This part of the training program will be made into a PowerPoint presentation with voiceover that could be used for future staff development training programs. Protocol Cards, developed by AMDA for use by LTC nurses, are designed to facilitate the gathering and presentation of information during physician phone calls. The 15 most common clinical problems, for example, pain and agitation, and their protocol cards will be included in a handout. The AMDA protocol cards will be reviewed, and an example, using one card to evaluate a clinical problem, will be demonstrated. A survey measuring nurse satisfaction with telephone communication (10 items) will be administered to LTC nurses before the program, immediately post program, and 4 to 6 weeks after instruction. A Wilcoxon sign rank test will be used to assess for differences.

E

Evidence Generating: Learning From Practitioner Owners of Clinics in Missouri

PROPOSAL ABSTRACT – PAULA ISRAEL

BACKGROUND

In Missouri, a collaborative practice agreement is required for nurse practitioners (NPs) to deliver care. Delegated tasks are more restrictive than what is possible based on education and scope of practice granted by the state board of nursing. In addition, limitations are imposed by legislators in Missouri.

SIGNIFICANCE

A dearth of providers has created unprecedented opportunities for NPs. Existing literature cites limited autonomy, reduced rates of reimbursement, incongruent state practice acts, and lack of business acumen as barriers to independent NP clinic ownership. NPs are identified as one viable solution to the lack of primary care providers in the United States.

PURPOSE

Opportunities and barriers to NP-owned clinics will be explored through the review of the literature and by description of experiences of NP clinic owners in one Midwestern state.

THEORY

Donabedian's theory of structure, process, and outcomes provides a framework for this project. Regulations and reimbursement (structure) allowing NPs to practice to the full extent of their training (process) could increase health care access (outcome) for Missourians.

METHODS

This will be a descriptive, exploratory study of NP clinic owners. An online survey, consisting of 11 open-ended and 4 structured questions, was developed from the literature and insights were gained from observing one business owner's patterns and practices. Fourteen of 19 identified clinic owners will meet inclusion criteria and be invited to describe their experience through self-report.

ANALYSIS

Descriptive analysis will include a summary of participant characteristics. Content analysis of qualitative data responses will be completed seeking key themes. Implications for practice, policy, education, and research will be generated from the findings.

References

Academic Center for Evidence-Based Practice. (2013). *ACE star model of knowledge transformation*. Retrieved from http://www.acestar.uthscsa.edu/acestar-model.asp

American Association of Colleges of Nursing. (2006). *The essentials of doctoral education for advanced nursing practice*. Retrieved from http://www.aacn.nche.edu/dnp/pdf/essentials.pdf

American Association of Higher Education. (n.d.). *Nine principles of good practice for assessing student learning*. Retrieved from http://www.dartmouth.edu/~oir/assessmenteval/tools/9principles.html

American Library Association. (2009). *Information literacy competency standards for higher education*. Retrieved from http://www.ala.org/acrl/standards/informationliteracycompetency

American Medical Directors Association. (2009). *Caregiver's communication guide: Protocols for change of condition*. Columbia, MD: Author.

American Nurses Association. (2010). *Scope and standards of practice* (2nd ed.). Silver Spring, MD: Author.

American Psychological Association. (2010). *Publication manual of the American Psychological Association* (6th ed.). Washington, DC: Author.

Berg, B. (2008) *Qualitative research methods for the social sciences* (7th ed.). Boston, MA: Pearson Publishing.

Bolker, J. (1998). *Writing your dissertation in fifteen minutes a day: A guide to starting, revising, and finishing your doctoral thesis*. Brighton, Victoria, Australia: Owl Publishing.

Bonnel, D. (2011). *Physical therapist assistant students' attitudes towards electronic health records*. (unpublished senior project). Washburn University, Topeka, KS.

Bonnel, M. (2012). *The room safety scan project* (unpublished course paper). Fort Hays State University, Hays, KS.

Bonnel, W. (1993). Managing the work of eating: The nursing home group dining experience. *Journal of Nutrition for the Elderly, 13*(1), 1–10.

Bonnel, W. (1996). Not gone and not forgotten, a spouse's experience of late stage Alzheimer's disease caregiving. *Journal of Psychosocial Nursing, 34*(8), 23–27.

Bonnel, W., Belt, J., Hill, D., Wiggins, S., & Ohm, R. (2000). Challenges and strategies for initiating a nursing facility practice. *Journal of the American Academy of Nurse Practitioners, 12*(9), 353–359.

Bonnel, W., & Boehm, H. (2011). Faculty practices in providing online course feedback. *Journal of Continuing Nursing Education, 42*(11), 503–509.

Boyer, E. L. (1990). *Scholarship reconsidered: Priorities of the professoriate.* Princeton, NJ: Carnegie Foundation for the Advancement of Teaching.

Brewer, T. L. (2009). *Pediatric nurses' attitudes and knowledge regarding the provision of breastfeeding support in a pediatric medical center.* Retrieved from http://www .doctorsofnursingpractice.org/studentprojects.php

Cambridge Rindge & Latin School. (2009). *Writing a statement of purpose.* Retrieved December 11, 2012, from http://www.crlsresearchguide.org/09_writing_ state_of_purp.asp

Chinn, P. L., & Kramer, M. K. (2011). *Integrated theory and knowledge development in nursing* (8th ed.). St. Louis, MO: Elsevier Mosby.

Coley, S., & Scheinberg, C. (2007). *Proposal writing: Effective grantsmanship.* New York, NY: Sage.

Cronenwett, L., Sherwood, G., Pohl, J., Barnsteiner, J., Moore, S., Sullivan, D. T., . . . Warren, J. (2009). Quality and safety education for advanced nursing practice. *Nursing Outlook, 57*(6), 338–348.

Duke University. (2005). *Patient safety—quality improvement.* Retrieved from http:// patientsafetyed.duhs.duke.edu/index.html

Dunsford, J. (2009). Structured communication: Improving patient safety with SBAR. *Nursing for Women's Health, 13*(5), 384–390.

Dusick, D. M. (2011). *Bold educational software: Writing the purpose statement.* Retrieved December 11, 2012, from http://bold-ed.com/purpose.htm

Evangelista-Hoffman, E. (2009). *Emergency department (ED) sepsis care: Application of the Iowa Model of Evidence Based Practice (EBP).* Retrieved from http://www .doctorsofnursingpractice.org/studentprojects.php

Federal Policy for the Protection of Human Subjects. (2010). 45 CFR 46, subpart A. Retrieved from http://www.hhs.gov/ohrp/humansubjects/guidance/45cfr46 .html

Filaskovsky, J. M. (2007). *Effect of an intervention to increase knowledge of the danger of delay in seeking treatment for chest pain.* Retrieved from http://www.doctorsofnursing practice.org/studentprojects.php

Fink, A. (2004). *Evaluation fundamentals: Insights into the outcomes, effectiveness, and quality of health programs.* New York, NY: Sage.

Fink, A. (2009). *Conducting research literature reviews: From the Internet to paper* (3rd ed.). Thousand Oaks, CA: Sage.

Galvan, J. (2006). *Writing literature reviews: A guide for students of the behavioral sciences* (3rd ed.). Glendale, CA: Pyrczak Publishing.

Garrard, J. (2010). *Health sciences literature review made easy: The matrix method* (3rd ed.). Boston, MA: Jones & Bartlett.

Halon, P. A. (2011). *Improving depression screening, diagnosis, and treatment in a diverse urban university health service.* Retrieved from http://www .doctorsofnursingpractice.org/studentprojects.php

Hayne, A. N. (2011). *Using problem based learning to analyze health policy.* Retrieved from http://www.doctorsofnursingpractice.org/studentprojects.php

Hober, C. (2012). *Student perceptions of the observer role play experiences in the imple- mentation of a high fidelity patient simulation in bachelor's degree nursing programs.*

Dissertation, University of Kansas. Retrieved from http://kuscholarworks .ku.edu/dspace/bitstream/1808/9981/1/Hober_ku_0099D_11950_DATA_ 1.pdf

Huber, M., & Hutchings, P. (2005). *The advancement of learning: Building the teaching commons.* San Francisco, CA: Jossey-Bass.

Hutchings, P. (2002). *The scholarship of teaching and learning in higher education preface.* Retrieved from http://www.carnegiefoundation.org/sites/default/files/ CASTL_bibliography.pdf

Institute of Medicine. (2011). *The future of nursing: Leading change, advancing health.* Washington, DC: The National Academies Press.

Institute of Medicine. (2012). *Living well with chronic illness: A call for public health action.* Washington, DC: The National Academies Press.

Institute of Medicine Committee on the Health Professions Education. (2003). *Health professions education: A bridge to quality.* Washington, DC: The National Academies Press.

Interprofessional Education Collaborative. (2011). *Core competencies for interprofessional collaborative practice.* Retrieved from http://www.aacn.nche.edu/ education-resources/ipecreport.pdf

Interprofessional Education Collaborative Expert Panel. (2011). *Core competencies for interprofessional collaborative practice: Report of an expert panel.* Washington, DC: Interprofessional Education Collaborative.

Jacobs, S. K., Rosenfeld, P., & Haber, J. (2003). Information literacy as the foundation for evidence-based practice in graduate nursing education: A curriculum-integrated approach. *Journal of Professional Nursing, 19*(5), 320–328.

Krathwohl, D., & Smith, N. (2005). *How to prepare a dissertation proposal: Suggestions for students in education and the social and behavioral sciences.* Syracuse, NY: Syracuse University Press.

Leedy, P., & Omrod, J. (2013). *Practical research: Planning and design* (10th ed.). Boston, MA: Pearson.

Mansfield, R. (2010). *Using glucose patterns to improve diabetes management in long-term care.* Presentation to the Gerontological Advanced Practice Nurses' Association. Albuquerque, NM.

McEwen, M., & Wills, W. M. (2011). *Theoretical basis for nursing* (3rd ed.). Philadelphia, PA: Wolters Kluwer & Lippincott Williams & Wilkins.

McNamara, C. (n.d.). *Basic guide to outcomes-based evaluation for nonprofit organizations with very limited resources.* Retrieved from http://managementhelp .org/evaluation/outcomes-evaluation-guide.htm

Meleis, A. I. (2012). *Theoretical nursing development & progress* (5th ed.). Philadelphia, PA: Wolters Kluwer & Lippincott Williams & Wilkins.

Melnyk, B. M., & Fineout-Overholt, E. (2011). *Evidence-based practice in nursing & healthcare* (2nd ed.). Philadelphia, PA: Wolters Kluwer, Lippincott Williams & Wilkins.

Morton, A. (2012). What nurses need to know about sleep apnea. *Nursing Made Incredibly Easy, 10*(3), 34–42.

Nelson, J., & Watson, J. (2011). *Measuring caring: International research on caritas as healing.* New York, NY: Springer Publishing Company.

Oermann, M., & Hays, H. (2011). *Writing for publication in nursing* (2nd ed.). New York, NY: Springer Publishing Company.

Peterson, J. M. (2009). *Using the transtheoretical model in primary care weight management: Tipping the decisional balance scale for exercise.* Retrieved from http://www.doctorsofnursingpractice.org/studentprojects.php

Peterson, S. J., & Bredow, T. S. (2013). *Middle range theories: Application to nursing research* (3rd ed.). Philadelphia, PA: Wolters Kluwer & Lippincott Williams & Wilkins.

Polit, D., & Beck, C. T. (2012). *Nursing research generating and assessing evidence for nursing practice* (8th ed.). Baltimore, MD: Lippincott, Williams, & Wilkins.

Rice, J., & Haycraft, K. (2012). Applying Lean and Six Sigma to your dermatology practice. *Journal of the Dermatology Nurses' Association, 4*(2), 136–142.

Robinson, W. (2010). *The research problem statement.* Retrieved from http://web.utk.edu/~wrobinso/540_lec_problem.html

Salkind, N. (2011). *Statistics for people who think they hate statistics.* Thousand Oaks, CA: Sage.

Sanchez, I. (2010). *Implementation of diabetes self-management education using shared medical appointments in primary care for adults.* Retrieved from http://www.doctorsofnursingpractice.org/studentprojects.php

San Francisco Edits. (n.d.). *Fourteen steps to writing an effective discussion section.* Retrieved from http://www.sfedit.net/discussion.pdf

Santucci, S. (2010). *A system change: Expansion of primary and secondary HIV prevention in a marginalized community.* Retrieved from http://www.doctorsofnursingpractice.org/studentprojects.php

Savers, C. (2011). *Anatomy of writing for publication for nurses.* Indianapolis, IN: Sigma Theta Tau International.

Standards for Quality Improvement Reporting Excellence. (n.d.). *Squire guidelines summary.* Retrieved from http://squire-statement.org/guidelines

Steneck, N. H. (2007). *Office of research integrity: Introduction to the responsible conduct of research.* Retrieved from http://ori.hhs.gov/documents/rcrintro.pdf

U.S. Department of Health and Human Services. (2011). *Report to Congress: National strategy for quality improvement in health care.* Retrieved from http://www.healthcare.gov/news/reports/nationalqualitystrategy032011.pdf

U.S. Department of Health and Human Services, Centers for Disease Control and Prevention. (2009). *The obesity epidemic and United States students.* Retrieved from www.cdc.gov/HealthyYouth/yrbs/pdf/yrbs07_us_obesity.pdf

Walker, L., & Avant, K. (2011). *Strategies for theory construction in nursing* (5th ed.). Boston, MA: Prentice Hall.

Walker, S., Sechrist, K., & Pender, N. (1987). The health-promoting lifestyle profile: Development and psychometric characteristics. *Nursing Research, 36*(2), 76–81.

Warren, C. & Karner, T. (2005). *Discovering qualitative methods: Field research, interviews, and analysis.* Oxford: Oxford University Press.

Whitman, G. (2003). What patient outcome should our outcomes management team measure? *Outcomes Management, 7*(3), 94–96.

Wolcott, H. (2008). *Writing up qualitative research*. Thousand Oaks, CA: Sage.

World Health Organization. (2009). *Global strategy on diet, physical activity and health. Childhood overweight and obesity. Childhood overweight and obesity on the rise.* Retrieved from http://www.who.int/dietphysicalactivity/childhood/en

Zachary, L. J. (2000). *The mentor's guide: Facilitating effective learning relationships.* San Francisco, CA: Jossey-Bass.

Index